THE BEGGAR'S BANQUET

A Personal Retreat on Christ, His Mother,
the Spiritual Life, and the Saints

THE
BEGGAR'S
BANQUET

A Personal Retreat on Christ, His Mother,
the Spiritual Life, and the Saints

REGIS MARTIN

EMMAUS
ROAD
PUBLISHING

Steubenville, Ohio
A Division of Catholics United for the Faith
www.emmausroad.org

Emmaus Road Publishing
827 North Fourth Street
Steubenville, Ohio 43952

Library of Congress Control Number: 2013953991
ISBN: 978-1-940329-14-7

Cover design and layout by: Theresa Westling

Cover art: Gianni Dagli Orti / The Art Archive at Art Resource, NY
Chicken, still life, paint on wood, 1639 / Binoit. Peter (fl. 1611-1624)

For Roseanne

Man never stops seeking: both when he is marked by the drama of violence, loneliness, and insignificance, and when he lives in serenity and joy, he continues to seek. The only answer which can satisfy him and appease this search of his comes from the encounter with the One who is at the source of his being and his action. The road is Christ. He is the Way, the Truth, and the Life, who reaches the person in his day-to-day existence. The discovery of this road normally comes about through the mediation of other human beings. Christianity, even before being a sum of doctrines or a rule of salvation, is thus the "event" of an encounter.

—Pope John Paul II, "Letter to Msgr. Luigi Giussani on the Occasion of the 50th Anniversary of the Movement 'Communion and Liberation,'" February, 22, 2004

Being Christian is not the result of an ethical choice or a lofty idea, but the encounter with an event, a person, which gives life a new horizon and a decisive direction.

—Pope Benedict XVI, *Deus caritas est*, 1

The Faith is not given us in order that we preserve it, but in order that we communicate it. If we don't have the passion to communicate it, we don't preserve it.

—Luigi Giussani, Testimony before the XXI Plenary Assembly of the Pontifical Council for the Laity, 2004

CONTENTS

PREFACE

It was the morning of the last day, and the driver, his engine idling in the frozen air, was waiting to whisk me off the mountain down into the valley far below, to a world very different from the stillness and peace I had come to experience amid the high and silent hills surrounding the Abbey of the Holy Trinity. I had just finished giving my final conference when, out of the blue, it hit me that I might actually try and make a little book of these reflections. I had been asked to come all this way to Utah to give them, and the monks, God bless them, managed triumphantly to survive the ordeal, so why not transcribe them into something less fleeting than the snows of yesteryear?

In point of fact, a baker's dozen had been delivered, given twice each day to a wonderfully captive audience over the course of a week, their length exactingly held to twenty-five blessed minutes apiece. "The monks are very old," the genial Abbot informed me over the phone (who, it turns out, was fairly long in the tooth himself), "and they may not stay awake if you go on too long." I understood perfectly. Hadn't my wife and children been telling me for years to stop talking? Excellent advice. Besides, if one were regularly required to leap out of bed at 3:00 a.m., who wouldn't fall asleep?

Arrangements were duly made for the first week in January, during which I would be expected to edify an eager if aging community of nearly twenty Cistercian monks, their beautifully sequestered setting nestled beneath a series of steeply wooded slopes some fifty miles outside Salt Lake City.

About what? My initial answer came swiftly to mind. *Silence*. God's first language. What better threads to weave together than those mysteriously wrapped about the world of silence? I would start at once. However, in my first innocence I had quite forgotten one or two things. To begin with, I knew almost nothing of silence, save only that there is never enough of it amid the crowded circumstances of my life. Where and when is a father of ten children, teacher of hundreds of students, to find time to enter that privileged realm?

Where shall the word be found, where will the word
Resound? Not here, there is not enough silence
(T. S. Eliot, "Ash Wednesday,"
written in 1930 following his
conversion to Christianity.)[1]

And—point two—who was I to tell men steeped in traditions stretching back twelve uninterrupted centuries or more about the very medium in which their whole lives are spent? It would have been the sheerest presumption. I'd have just as soon set about catechizing fish on the mysteries of water.

Was there another topic I could come up with? Something about which I should not need to feel entirely mortified to speak? A subject, moreover, of absolute, riveting importance? I should not dream of traveling thousands of miles to a remote monastery in order to play the dilettante to serious men determined on the life of holiness. The choice was obvious. I would speak of the Mystery of Jesus. And, of course, Mary, the Church, and the saints, and ourselves in living relation to them. A tall order, to be sure, but worth the effort.

What follows is a series of meditations, then, whose single aim is to illumine the mind, to mobilize the heart, so that the reader may be moved to engage the God who has first come among us for our salvation. To give God permission, as it were, to enter our lives in order then to draw us straight to His heart. Because we are beings most profoundly and precisely made for God, heaven must become the deepest desire we have. Do we have that relish for eternal life? May it please God to possess us more and more each day. And may these few pages help to feed that hunger.

I have tried to preserve the spoken quality of the experience so that, as nearly as possible, what you are holding in your hands is a faithful rendering of the talks as I delivered them to the holy men who kindly came to hear them. Some liberties of course have been taken to improve the quality of the prose, to move it along in ways more agreeably literary. But these have been few and designed to improve the flow of the narrative.

I offer these pages to my wife, who, for all that she was obliged to give up in order for me to go to Utah, never faltered in urging me to get on with it.

---

1. *The Complete Poems and Plays 1909–1950* (New York: Harcourt, Brace & World, Inc., 1971), 65.

DISPELLING THE DARKNESS

Thank you for coming. I am honored and delighted to be here. Of course I don't know what options *you* had. Perhaps you were free to choose between me or going back to bed . . . in which case I'm awfully grateful you've elected to stay awake. I shall certainly endeavor to keep you that way.

Why don't we begin with a prayer, asking God to bless this time we spend together. A simple *Our Father*, followed by a brief invocation to the Holy Spirit, seems sufficient to launch this modest enterprise.

By the way, I always tell my students on the first day that I'd like to begin all my classes that way. And that those of atheist persuasion who choose to object can just go and offer it up. It will do their souls no end of good.

They all laugh, of course, since there are no atheists among the students I teach, which is one of the more endearing features of Franciscan University of Steubenville. At least none who have made any sort of public profession. On the other hand, it is not my business to expose the theological eccentricities of my students, whom I've no doubt would be rightly horrified were I (or anyone else for that matter) to draw attention to this or that aberration of unbelief. But, happily enough, most of my students appear to be both sane and pious, unlike so many young people these days who, on first leaving home, often fall headlong into apostasy.

Not a few of my students, in fact, seem to have fallen headlong in love with Jesus Christ, for whom they long to make huge and heroic sacrifices. It is, I tell you, a very humbling experience to be talking about God to young people, so many of whom are already deeply and intimately involved with Him. On the other hand, I do sometimes wish my students were perhaps slightly less pious, as it would give me something to measure my skills against. Having an atheist or two in class is more than a provocation: it is a challenge.

It also helps the rest of us from becoming too smug, a point Joseph Ratzinger once made in a splendid book he wrote back in the 1960s. It was, you may remember, the height of the Silly Season, and the so-called Death of God Movement was in high gear, becoming something of a fashion statement among the wise and the clever. An entire theology had grown up around that particular nonsense, as if it were ever possible to dagger God to death. Anyway, he wrote this terrific book called *Introduction to Christianity*,[1] which so captivated the pope (Paul VI) that practically on the strength of its charm and conviction he made him a bishop. An Archbishop, in fact, of Munich, which thereupon became a sort of launching pad for an elevation that would prove swiftly and surprisingly meteoric. So quickly did this shy young bookish Bavarian priest/professor climb the episcopal ladder that, as God would have it, within a few short years he would become the most important figure in the Church. Certainly he has become someone whose original and compelling vision of God, the world, and the crucial importance of faith in it, has galvanized many in the Church, becoming indeed a source of inspiration to millions.

Well, it all began with a single book written more than forty years ago. Ideas surely do have consequences. A book that would not only make him famous; it would make me a theologian. I cut my teeth on that text, which I now gleefully inflict upon my students.

What Ratzinger aims to do in this book, he tells us, is to provide an analysis of why modern man finds it so difficult to believe, to bring himself to profess any sort of lively faith in God. Citing what he calls the sheer "oppressive power of unbelief in the midst of one's own will to believe," he reminds us that the believer is always threatened, always beset and bedeviled by the "strangeness and insecurity of his own faith," an uncertainty which, "in moments of temptation can suddenly and unexpectedly cast a piercing light on the fragility of the whole that usually seems so self-evident to him."[2]

---

1. New York: The Seabury Press, 1969.
2. Ibid., 17.

Here the example of the Little Flower comes sharply to mind. "That lovable saint," he calls her, "who looks so naïve and unproblematical, had grown up in an atmosphere of complete religious security; her whole existence from beginning to end, and down to the smallest detail, was so completely molded by the faith of the Church that the invisible world had become not just part of her everyday life, but that life itself."[3]

So wonderfully palpable were the structures of her faith, Ratzinger tells us, so utterly tangible that religious cocoon in which she felt herself to be perfectly snug and secure, that not even thought itself could pry her loose. "To her, 'religion' really was a self-evident presupposition of her daily existence; she dealt with it as we deal with the concrete details of our lives. Yet this very saint . . . left behind her, from the last weeks of her passion, shattering admissions which her horrified sisters toned down in her literary remains and which have only now come to light in the new verbatim editions. She says, for example, 'I am assailed by the worst temptations of atheism.' Everything has become questionable, everything is dark. She feels tempted to take only the sheer void for granted."[4]

Now that certainly is an ice-breaker. One surely does not expect Arctic blasts of atheism to come sweeping across the landscape *of her* soul. And yet here unmistakably was hard evidence of Thérèse's Dark Night, threatening to extinguish any possible flame of light or hope. "In other words," Joseph Ratzinger continues his remorseless probing of the terrible siege of her soul, "in what is apparently a flawlessly interlocking world someone here suddenly catches a glimpse of the abyss lurking—even for her—under the firm structure of the supporting conventions."[5]

Tormented thus by doubt and despair, poor Thérèse must make her way across a great and terrible sea of nihilism, without a single resource of conventional piety, it would seem, on which she might confidently depend. "In a situation like this," explains Ratzinger, "what is in question is not the sort of thing that one perhaps quarrels about otherwise—the dogma of the Assumption, the proper use of confession—all this becomes absolutely secondary. What is at stake is the whole structure; it is a question of all or nothing. That is the only remaining alternative; nowhere does there seem anything to cling to in this sudden fall. All that can be seen is the bottomless depths of the void into which one is also staring."[6]

---

3. Ibid., 17.
4. Ibid., 17–18.
5. Ibid., 18.
6. Ibid., 18.

What nonsense to think of her as this woefully sheltered sister, full of child-ish and romantic fancies; this dreadfully dull, shy, timid specimen of nineteenth century neurotic religiosity! She was not at all like that. She was positively heroic. Indeed, she entered into, from the very depths of her own interiority, the whole vertiginous drama of modern atheist despair, but without giving in to it one tiny bit. Her experience of the hellishness of the absence of God was more profound, more terrifying even, than anything found in that mad-man Nietzsche.

Her descriptions of the encircling darkness in the days and weeks before her death testify, in an almost unsurpassed way, to the terrible ordeal of the nihilism of our time; yet they do so precisely because, in the dark night of her hope, she rises triumphantly above them. The very darkness, she tells us, "borrowing the voice of sinners, says mockingly to me, 'You are dreaming about the light; about a country fragrant with sweetest perfumes . . . about the eternal possession of the Creator of all these things; you believe that one day you will walk out of this fog which surrounds you! Dream on, dream on; rejoice in death which will give you not what you hope for, but even deeper night, the night of nothingness.'"[7]

But she did not listen to the darkness, refusing to heed the devil's summons to a despair without end. She simply would not give in, yielding up her spirit to the allure of the abyss, the hell of an eternity without love, without God. Her final words put to rest that damnable lie. "My God," she says simply, "I love you."[8]

Let us put on the faith and the hope of the Little Flower, this valiant Saint of the Holy Face, Thérèse of Lisieux, Doctor of the Church; and armed thus with the grace of the power of Christ's presence—yes, even when we feel only His absence—walk toward that seeming darkness full of light and courage, and, as always, under the aspect of supernatural hope, the certainty of salvation.

---

7. Guy Gaucher, *The Story of a Life* (San Francisco: Harper & Row, 1987), 161. It is an account, masterfully told, of St. Thérèse's life, sufferings, and death.
8. Ibid., 205.

MAN AS PURE SEARCH

I begin with a story told by Monsignor Luigi Giussani, founder of *Communion and Liberation*, a movement that has mushroomed in recent years, particularly among young people for whom the hunger and thirst for God, for ultimate truth and beauty and happiness, cries out for that fulfillment which only Christ can bring. It is a story he has recounted in several places, including at the very end of his book, *The Religious Sense*.[1] It provides an ideal point of entry for a reflection on what Blaise Pascal has called "the Mystery of Jesus."

The details of the story, he tells us, touch on an experience he had many years before, an experience whose impact would prove so immense and far-reaching that it became the defining theme of his life, his work. It amounted to a sort of signature statement, a benchmark to identify, to summarize, the meaning of his being.

"Once, as a very young man," he begins, "I got lost in the great wood of Tradate . . . and, in the grip of panic, I shouted for a full three hours as the sun sank in the sky. That experience made me see—afterwards—that man is search; man is search if he cries out . . ."[2]

---

1. *The Religious Sense*, trans. John Zucchi (Montreal & Kingston, London, Buffalo: McGill-Queen's University Press, 1997).
2. Ibid., 144.

Now I haven't a clue as to what or where this forest of Tradate is (perhaps it is in the north of Italy, near Milan, the region where he was born); but I suspect it must be a deep and dark and dense forest, a wholly sinister setting in which to be lost. And, to be sure, only an Italian is capable of producing three hours of full-throated shouting.

But where is Giussani going with this? What is he getting at? Only this: That to be human, to aspire to the meaning of what fundamentally defines our humanity, is to be someone whose whole life can only be understood in terms of *search*. That, it seems to me, is axiomatic. Life understood as search, as quest. To be alive, in other words, is always to have this eagerness to explore, to seek, to study, to find out. Life as sheer hunger and thirst. Man, says Plato, is a child of poverty. The plate is always empty.

All of which, of course, leads one to ask if there is some reason to justify the search. One does not ordinarily embark upon an empty quest. So what is the reason? It is the fact that you are quite simply lost. And the sudden realization of that fact, of the bloody fix you're in, puts you at once in the throes of a panic. So you cry out. What else can you do? Your situation is exactly parallel to that of the great Dante, the premier pilgrim-poet of the Christian world, who, finding himself alone in the Dark Wood in the middle of the journey of *his* life, is likewise moved to cry out. It is the afternoon of Good Friday in the year 1300 and he is 35 years of age. "Midway in our life's journey," he tells us on the very first page of the *Divine Comedy*, "I went astray from the straight road and woke to find myself / Alone in a dark wood. How shall I say / what wood that was! I never saw so drear, so rank, so arduous a wilderness! / Its very memory gives a shape to fear. / Death could scarce be more bitter than that place!"[3]

So you have got to cry out, to externalize the fear, in order to find out where you are. You can't keep it to yourself. In short, each of us is a kind of castaway, who perhaps by some strange mis-chance of fate, a bout of bad *karma* as it were, has fallen from the sky. I think of that silly Tom Hanks movie (thanks to the privations of monastic life you were doubtless spared having to watch it) which shows some poor guy literally falling out of an airplane onto a beach where, among other absurdities, he develops a relationship with a volleyball.[4]

Not recommended.

---

3. *The Divine Comedy*, trans. John Ciardi (New York: New American Library, 1954). See "The Inferno," first of three epic journeys (hell, purgatory, paradise), Canto I, 28.
4. *Cast Away* is a 2000 American film about a FedEx employee stranded on an uninhabited island after his plane crashed in the South Pacific.

Or put it this way: man is a beggar ("the true protagonist of history," Giussani calls him),[5] who must cry out for all that he does not have. It is not that his glass is half-full; the glass is empty. And amid "the parched eviscerate soil" (T. S. Eliot, "Little Gidding"),[6] his roots need rain. But he cannot stifle the cry. Lest it leave him strangled in his very soul, he must declaim his hunger and thirst. He trumpets it to the heavens. Yes, even if, as Shakespeare puts it, his cries be "bootless."

> When in disgrace with fortune and men's eyes,
> I all alone beweep my outcast state,
> And trouble deaf heaven with my bootless cries . . .
> (Sonnet 29)

Ah, but there is another and still deeper consideration at work here. The experience of being lost—seemingly, hopelessly, forever—that experience, says Giussani, besides revealing man as pure search—as one the whole thrust of whose being simply must cry out—testifies at the same time to a real if mysterious certainty of *Another*. There is this real intimation, you see, of the presence of someone who can actually hear the cry of the poor. "The cry implies the existence of something other," he tells us. Otherwise, why would man cry out at all?

Is that clear? If nobody is there, why on earth would you cry out? It is quite horrible enough just being frightened out of ones's skin. But to be foolish as well is entirely too off-putting. "The very existence of the question," says Giussani, "implies the existence of an answer."[7] And why is that? Because, "expectation is the very structure of our nature, it is the essence of our soul. It is not something calculated: it is given. For the promise is at the origin, from the very origin of our creation. He who has made man has also made him as 'promise.' Structurally man waits; structurally he is a beggar; structurally life is promise."[8]

Isn't this finally the reason why there must be a God, why this insistent, desperate desire will someday, someway, find fulfillment? That all the questions put to what appears to be only a blank and indifferent sky will, nevertheless, be finally answered in the *You of Another*? "Thus Faith," Joseph Ratzinger reminds

---

5. "Existence expresses itself, as ultimate ideal, in begging. The real protagonist of history is the beggar: Christ who begs for man's heart, and man's heart that begs for Christ" (Testimony before John Paul II, 1998).
6. *Four Quartets* from *Collected Poems*, 140. "The parched eviscerate soil / Gapes at the vanity of toil."
7. *The Religious Sense*, 58.
8. Ibid., 54.

us, "is the finding of a 'you' that bears me up and amid all the unfulfilled—and in the last resort unfulfillable—hope of human encounters gives me the promise of an indestructible love which not only longs for eternity but guarantees it. Christian faith lives on the discovery that not only is there such a thing as objective meaning, but this meaning knows me and loves me, I can entrust myself to it like the child that knows all its questions answered in the 'you' of its mother."[9]

In other words, there is an answer to this cry; indeed, the more desperate the cry for help, the more certain we are of an answer. But the answer does not come out of any sort of thing we might devise (a compass, say), whose usefulness is seen at once to be equal to the predicament we're in. The state of being lost is simply not amenable to solution in human terms. Escape can only come, I am saying, from the outside, from above. From a source both transcendent to the mess, that is, *One* who is Himself not lost; and yet, having submitted Himself to a state of being lost, is thus able to identify with His lost brother and so effect the rescue our hearts cry out for. We are all lost. There are no exceptions to the desolation we experience, the fearful desperation it inflicts. And it is only the Event of Jesus Christ, who comes into the flesh of sin in order precisely to free us from its malice and misery, that can lift us finally onto the plane of grace and glory.

There is one final point, which is the most startling of all. And that is the fact that the very nature of the rescue offered by Christ, when it erupts into our world, bursting through the ceiling of our lives, all at once exceeds every conceivable expectation we have that—somehow, someway—we shall be saved. What this means is that a life sustained by hope, a life whose scaffolding rests upon the expectation that everything will turn out well in the end ("Sin is behovely, but all shall be well, and all shall be well and all manner of thing shall be well,")[10] suddenly and unaccountably discovers a fulfillment totally surpassing even the highest and loftiest possibilities of human expectation.

> I did not know my longing, till I encountered You.
> I see what freedom is; Your plan prepared for me.
> I will not search for more because
> You will save me now.[11]

---

9. *Introduction to Christianity*, 48.
10. From Julian of Norwich's *Sixteen Revelations of Divine Love*, fourteenth century.
11. From a hymn entitled *Il Disegno* (The Design), used by members of Communion and Liberation.

The castaway, you see, is *Everyman*. Or, at the very least, that man who possesses by some inscrutable grace the certainty of the awareness that he is a castaway, lost in the great forest of being, yet strangely aware of a way out. The very path Christ Himself having first blazed through that forest, the rest of us are now free to follow.

Christianity, then, is really nothing other than an event that each of us is meant to encounter. It is a radically new and unforeseen happening in the great sea of history. And, to be sure, what is most symptomatic about it, the feature that fairly leaps off the page, is the discovery we make that precisely in Christ, in the human form assumed by God, we see and experience the pure mercy of Our Father in Heaven.

I leave you with this lovely and expressive passage from St. Augustine in his Exposition on Psalm 71.

> You were walking in your own way, a vagabond straying
> through wooded places, through rugged places, torn in all
> your limbs. You were seeking a home and you did not find
> it. There came to you the way itself and you were set therein.
> Walk by Him, the Man, and you come to God.

IN HIS IMAGE AND LIKENESS

The desire for God, it has often and wisely been observed, is written on the human heart. It is a kind of inscription, or imprint, telling us who we are; an image or template, as it were, impressed upon the soul. Part of our spiritual DNA.

Well, what does that mean? Is there a presupposition here that we need to get a handle on? About God, certainly. But also about ourselves, those being the two pivotal words in the equation.

"When I was fifteen years of age," writes John Henry Newman in the story of his life, "a great change of thought took place in me. I fell under the influences of a definite Creed, and received into my intellect impressions of dogma which, through God's mercy, have never been effaced or obscured." What was the result of so definite and dogmatic an imprint? Nothing less, he tells us confidingly, than "making me rest in the thought of two and two only absolute and luminously self-evident beings, myself and my Creator . . ."[1]

So here are the two presuppositions at work, an unpacking of which may prove helpful in throwing light upon the spiritual life. The first is that it is perfectly natural for man to desire God, to wish to express this innate longing for Him, indeed, to be finally happy only in the arms of God. This is not

---

1. From his *Apologia Pro Vita Sua*, chapter 1, "History of My Religious Opinions to the Year 1833."

evidence of some vestigial organ whose removal would leave undisturbed the healthy functioning of the soul. No. It means that nothing will ultimately satisfy us unless, having been destined to be embraced for all eternity by the arms of the mystery of God, we in fact find our way home to heaven. This is nothing more than what Luigi Giussani has called "the religious sense," which you and I can no more escape than if it were possible actually to leap out of our own skin.

And it is not to be found in the first place at the level of grace, but of nature. That man evince this hunger and thirst, this longing for supernatural life, is simply a function of his being man. Because it is already inscribed in man's being to reach out and touch God, we do not require a special Revelation from on high to know this. It is simply and ineluctably a datum of human reason, human experience. In other words, it is a constitutive dimension of the creature we call man, which, were he to be divested of this desire, deprived therefore of all access to the God with whom he naturally desires to be united, a terrible and irreparable violence would be visited upon him. Nothing and no one could compensate him for a loss so necessary and fundamental to his well-being.

Nevertheless, it will require more than nature to consummate so natural and insistent a longing. While it may be true, as the Gospels tell us, that those who hunger for bread ought not to be given stones, it does not thereby follow that the hunger itself is what produces the bread. And so at every turn in the forest, behind every bush, there are perils awaiting us that only grace can enable us to face. To overcome. Nature cannot negotiate the road beyond nature, the journey that leads home to God. So we're all in a ditch—every "jack, joke, potsherd" among us, to evoke the image of Everyman found in that superb poem by Hopkins.[2] But free, entirely and blessedly free, to look up at the stars. And stare in sheer stupefied wonder at the heavens. So many "tortured wonders," to recall that lovely line from George Herbert.

> Once a poor creature, now a wonder,
> A wonder tortur'd in the space
> Betwixt this world and that of grace.
> (George Herbert, "Affliction," IV)

---

2. Gerard Manley Hopkins, "That Nature is a Heraclitean Fire and of the Comfort of the Resurrection," 22.

Thanks to the sheer graciousness of a God who need never have made us in the first place, we have all been invited to climb the ladder of sanctity that leads straight to Him.

What I am saying is that simply by virtue of one's being alive, that is, a sentient being who can both know and love, one is constrained to ask questions, questions of purest ultimacy. Who am I, for instance? Where have I come from? Where am I going? The answers to such questions throw open the window onto transcendence; they take us by the throat. And manifestly my being able to ask such questions demonstrates that this finite and continent creature must, out of some strange and unfathomable quirk of being, exist in real if mysterious relation to an infinite and necessary God.

> O that Thou shoulds't give dust a tongue
>   To crie to thee!
>   (George Herbert, "Denial")

What else does it mean for man to be a searcher, who, in tireless pursuit of an ultimate horizon of truth or beauty or justice, will not stop short, will not be satisfied, with anything less than the totality of reality? "The inability of the answer," says Giussani, "to satisfy the constitutive needs of our self is something structural; in other words, it is so inherent to our nature that it represents the very characteristic of our being."[3]

By the same token, then, it surely follows that there must be something quite extraordinary about God that He should wish to awaken such desires in the human heart. What would possess Him to plant and to nourish, and then to harvest, so profound and persisting a set of hungers? Not only must He be truth and power, but goodness and love as well. That between the two of us— the twin orders of God and man, grace and nature, heaven and history—there really does exist a kind of harmony, a correspondence, concerning which the only proper response is one of stunned gratitude and thanksgiving.

It is not, God forbid, a matter of identity; certainly God is not me or you or the world He made. We are not pantheists, who, in plucking leaves from our sleeves, are somehow discarding bits and pieces of God. And we are not to think of ourselves as being absorbed by God, either. Theopanism is no less repellent a prospect. But, on the other hand, the differences between us are not so pronounced as to reduce to enmity and division; God is not bent

---

3. *The Religious Sense*, 49.

on destroying the creature He fashioned in His image. Rather what we have got here is an analogical order consisting of the most wonderful and striking similarities; which at the same time, however, reveal still greater dissimilarities. While God and your retreat master share this kindred connection to being father—I to a family of ten and He to, well, who can number the children of God?—what remains yet more striking is the fact that His exercise of fatherhood is so radically and absolutely superior to my own poor performance.

What I am getting at is this: That when God shows Himself in, say, the work of creation, the job does not exhaust the infinite possibilities of God being God. And, really, isn't the whole tragic history of modern thought the result of its failure to hold these two things in tension? To refuse the twin polarities of God being both totally transcendent to the world He made and, at the same time, entirely present to that world? We are left to choose therefore between the *pathos* of so stressing the Absolute Otherness of God, the sheer Omnipotence of His crushing Will, as to rob the world of its reality. Or, on the other hand, allowing the world to somehow absorb God into itself as a result of too facile an identification of the two.

What rescues us from the two species of madness is precisely the fact that we are creatures made in God's image. Invited, therefore, through the life of grace to grow ever more into the likeness of God, which is made perfect in Christ Jesus. What else is sanctification but the journey we undertake from image to likeness? From the defilement of the image wrought by sin, to a divinization brought to perfection through our sharing in the very likeness of God. Disfigured by the one, transfigured by the other.

The Catechism of the Catholic Church speaks of the human soul as "the seed of eternity we bear in ourselves, which is irreducible to the merely material" (no. 33), and thus can have its origin only in One who stands above the material, that is, God. So, once again, we must acknowledge this basic thrust of the creature, evinced over and over in sheer *erotic* longing for One who alone can complete and fulfill the deepest driving desires of the heart. And everywhere you look, Augustine reminds us in that celebrated passage at the beginning of the *Confessions*, "the heart is restless until it finds rest in Thee." Each man, says Augustine, is this "hollowed-out space" only God can fill.[4] We are this marvelous musical instrument on which God wishes to play. Let us help Him tune the instrument so that together we might make beautiful music.

---

4. *Confessions*, Book One, Chapter 1.

Here is a splendid and instructive poem by George Herbert that sounds the same theme; it is called *The Pulley*.

> When God at first made man,
> Having a glass of blessings standing by—
> Let us (said He) pour on him all we can:
> Let the world's riches, which dispersed lie,
>> Contract into a span.
>
> So strength first made a way,
> Then beauty flow'd, then wisdom, honour, pleasure:
> When almost all was out, God made a stay,
> Perceiving that alone of all His treasure
>> Rest in the bottom lay.
>
> For if I should (said He)
> Bestow this jewel also on My creature,
> He would adore My gifts instead of Me,
> And rest in Nature, not the God of Nature:
>> So both should losers be.
>
> Yet let him keep the rest,
> But keep them with repining restlessness;
> Let him be rich and weary, that at least,
> If goodness lead him not, yet weariness
>> May toss him to My breast.[5]

So how does God proceed? With wonderful and ironic intent. He is perfectly willing, as He puts it, to let man be both rich and weary, "that at least / If goodness lead him not, yet weariness / May toss him to My breast." It is as if God were to say, "Look here, my child: I've given you everything; I've thrown all these perfections at you, and still you're not satisfied. So perhaps I shall just have to settle for less. Maybe only a weary resignation is the best We can do for you: A sort of terminal exhaustion will toss you at last onto Our lap!"

Let us then be grateful to God for showing such wit and patience before the impacted stubbornness of so many of His children. And try perhaps a little harder to love Him for Himself alone.

---

5. I quote this poem in its entirety in my collection, *Garlands of Grace: An Anthology of Great Christian Poetry* (San Francisco: Ignatius Press, 2002).

"THE INTOLERABLE WRESTLE
WITH WORDS AND MEANINGS"

Suppose we begin with two superbly instructive sentences, each spoken by a Church Father, both fraught with endless and rich promise for reflection. The first is Gregory of Nyssa telling us that, "If all things were within our grasp, the higher power would not be beyond us." The second is Gregory the Great reminding us that, "Almost everything said of God is unworthy, for the very reason that it is capable of being said."

For all their differences of temperament and tradition, the two nevertheless strike a common chord, a kindred note of understanding that turns on the Great Mystery itself, the architecture of the Christian God. Each is addressing the same God before whom we all stand in fear and trembling. Who is He and what has He left us that we need to know? The central shattering mystery of the absolute self-revealing God—is it possible to throw light upon Him?

Begin by asking what God intends when speaking to us, say, in the pages of Holy Scripture. Not so much what He is trying to tell us, but the fact that He should stoop to speak to us at all. Why does He do this? This is not the Book of Nature that God is writing across the pages of the cosmos, although that too is parabolic and so it will invariably signify more than it can say. What is being said here, however, in the precise context of the Bible, is meant to be revelatory of who God is in a far more complete and comprehensive way than any sort of cipher we use to parse the Book of Nature. So why does He speak to us in this special way?

It is because only here does God dare to speak the *Word,* the entirety of the Self-Utterance that is Himself. It is a Word none of us could ever speak. Not even a million years would be enough to come up with the absolutely right word (*le mot juste,* as they say in French). Indeed, for one to achieve perfect verbal adequacy before the self-revealing God, one would have to be God Himself. Aldous Huxley used to say that when placing a clever chimpanzee in front of a typewriter, one would have to be crazy to expect after a million or so years that it would manage to tap out the words of Hamlet's famous speech, "To be or not to be . . ." Imagine then the scale of difficulty were you or I to attempt to approximate God's own Word, God Himself? Who would dare to mount an exposition so impossible as that?

So God speaks the Word for us. And does so precisely for our salvation. *Pro nobis.* Those two tiny Latin words inserted into the ancient creed remind us that it was for our sake that Christ came down into the world, into the flesh of sin. And that the initiative for so daring and dramatic a descent belongs to God alone; it was not an idea that any of us could have thought up. "The framework of God's message to man in Christ," comments Hans Urs von Balthasar, "cannot be tied to the world in general, nor to man in particular; God's message is theological, or better theo-pragmatic. It is an act of God on man; an act done for and on behalf of man . . . and it is credible only as love . . . God's own love, the manifestation of which is . . . the glory of God."[1]

What this means, I think, is that whatever understanding we hope to possess as Christians, whether in pursuit of scholarship or, more importantly, discipleship, can only derive, finally, from the sheer self-glorification of eternal triune love, God's own love, which is God himself. *Agape,* love, is at the heart of all being, and that the two are to be seen entirely of a piece, wedded sublimely together, in a word, co-terminous. This love first appears in the *Kabod* of the Old Testament, which bespeaks the immensity of the glory of God, whose radiant, overwhelming presence spills over onto every page of scripture.

Even in the Old Testament, where the unheard of promises are first delivered to the People of the Book, and however long they must await His coming in the flesh, He does not stand aloof, hidden away amid an absolute *Otherness,*

---

1. *Love Alone: The Way of Revelation* (London: Burns & Oates Limited, 1968), 7–8.

but instead draws most fearfully close to the people He fashioned. He speaks to them, exacting a loyalty to His person, an observance of His laws that will brook neither opposition nor compromise. His Lordship and prerogatives thereof remain without question, beyond cavil. "For these reasons," writes Balthasar, "he is a God who in a terrifying, overwhelming manner becomes concrete for man—a God who, to put it another way, necessarily spreads anxiety."[2] In point of fact, the God of the Old Testament, precisely in the crushing weight of His divinity, the sheer overpowering presence of His majesty, "comes closer to man in the Old Covenant than in the New. He assails man unsparingly and snatches man to Himself with no preliminary courtship (this is done later, Balthasar reminds us, in His Incarnate Word). He manifests Himself in His Godhead so nakedly that man scarcely understands the love that is revealed in this impetuous ardor. Confused, man lowers his eyes and draws back, conscious of his sinful unworthiness. And so it seems as if God had wanted too much."[3]

Who will deliver man from the fire of such love? It is so devouring, so consuming that, as the prophets repeatedly tell us, no man may look upon the Lord God and live. Isaiah, for instance, thinks himself entirely lost having gazed upon the King with his own eyes. And Jacob, who wrestled long into the night with the Angel of the Lord, refusing to desist until he had extracted a blessing, will awaken upon a dreadful place that bespeaks the *Awful Haunter* of the universe. This is the God who first showed Himself to the people He aimed to save. "If he snatches up a man or a people to himself," Balthasar notes, "it is in a lightning-stroke of divine election, drawing the elect into the smoke and darkness of his divinity."[4] It is indeed a terrible thing to fall into the hands of the living God.

And when He comes at last in the flesh, what then happens? Why the whole weight of God's glory is all at once revealed in the love that is Jesus Christ, a love so astonishing that it wills to pursue the sinner to the very end, to the sheerest extremity of desolation and loss. Here is testimony indeed. To the deepest mystery of all, Christ's descent into hell, into the shame and the silence and the sorrow of *Sheol*. The Mystery of Holy Saturday, which the Church paradoxically locates at the center of the creed, the day on which all the tabernacles of Christendom are emptied of God and He appears to be truly dead. A love so boundless (it is literally without limit), a love whose constant

---

2. *The Christian and Anxiety* (San Francisco: Ignatius Press, 2000), 56.
3. Ibid., 56.
4. Ibid., 57.

and salient expression cries out for all the lost—all the unloved, the unlovely, the unloving—simply cannot be imagined or foreseen by anyone. And when it comes, this flash point erupting into time, the *Pleroma* of the Godhead spilling over into the *Kenosis* of the Son, it can only be understood ("perceived and received,"[5] says Balthasar) as the sheer and *Wholly Other*. Thus it must be God's own Word spoken in freedom and finality to man (and for man).

We must permit, I am saying, the self-revealing Word of God, the perfect and eternal Utterance, the very *Logos* of the Father, to be all that God wishes to be in each free and gracious disclosure of Himself. That, after all, is the whole purpose of Scripture: to speak the saving Word without either distortion or distraction. Let God be His own exegete. He provides both text and exegesis.

Otherwise, of course, the sacred text self-destructs before our very own eyes. And the meaning becomes a function of power or prejudice, a matter of sheer self-serving convenience. And not the truth of a God whose name is Truth, *Verbum*, Word, *Logos*.

What was it that the other Gregory sought to warn us about? "Almost everything said of God is unworthy, for the very reason that it is capable of being said." What else does he mean but that our words, which are finite and limited, must necessarily and painfully fall short of the divine reality to which they point. Human language will never rise to that level of adequacy perfectly congruent with God. Only God is equal to His Word. Like the asymptotic curve whose baseline the statistician may never reach, however much he seems to draw closer, so too must the gap remain between human language and divine *Logos*.

Dr. Samuel Johnson, in introducing his massive Dictionary, has beautifully parsed the point, comparing "the daughters of earth," which are the words we use, to "the sons of heaven," which are the things to which they point. And if despite your having sniffed out the faintest innuendo of male chauvinism here, you nevertheless steel yourself to follow the argument, you will acknowledge that the point really does survive the prejudice implicit in its expression. Alas, the shadow of finitude and flesh always and inevitably falls between the two.

How enormously, incalculably important the point is, too—testifying to what T. S. Eliot has called "the intolerable wrestle with words and meanings," which we humans are forced to undergo the moment we sense the separation between the truth we are obliged to speak and the bloody awkwardness of the language used to say it. "And so each new venture," Eliot reminds us,

---

5. *Love Alone*, 8.

Is a new beginning, a raid on the inarticulate
With shabby equipment always deteriorating
In the general mess of imprecision of feeling,
Undisciplined squads of emotion. And what there is to
    conquer
By strength and submission, has already been discovered
Once or twice, or several times, by men whom one cannot
    hope
To emulate—but there is no competition—
There is only the fight to recover what has been lost
And found and lost again and again: and now, under
    conditions
That seem unpropitious. But perhaps neither gain nor loss.
For us, there is only the trying. The rest is not our business.
                    (T. S. Eliot, Movement V of East Coker)[6]

Let us then turn to God, whose Word is totally and effortlessly adequate to
all that God is and wishes to say to the world, beseeching Him to teach us the
words we need, anointing their use in order to speak the full truth of who He
is and what He has done to save us.

---

6. The second of his *Four Quartets* from *Collected Poems*, 128.

"I AM AN ACCIDENT THAT HAPPENED TO HAPPEN"

What does it mean to be a creature? The usual dictionary definition is not entirely helpful since it tends more or less to repeat the word, that is, telling us that a creature is, well, something or someone created. That certainly would give the word an awful lot of mileage, including in its ambit every being from angels to amoebas. But that scarcely adds to the sum of human knowledge, does it?

So what does it really mean to be a creature? Does it mean anything more than merely being alive? In reaching for a bedrock definition, which is what the word requires if we're to get any sort of handle on the thing itself, it means to be someone or something whose existence is not at all necessary. An existence that is wholly contingent, accidental, as in the statement, "I am an accident that happened to happen." It means that one is not God. Only God is necessary, absolute, without antecedent cause. If it were to be shown that God needed something to set Him in motion, then He would not be God.

To be a creature then means to be given, from moment to moment, by Another, by God. Think of it this way: each of us is a word spoken by One who holds the entire alphabet of being in His mind. Were God to forget to speak this word that is me, the sacred syllables of my name, I should straightaway cease to exist. My whole life, therefore, is lived on borrowed being, on sufferance, on the capacity of Another to keep me alive, literally holding me above an abyss of nothingness.

So what does all that mean? What does it finally portend when each of us is constrained to say, I do not make myself, but instead, from moment to moment, receive my very self, all that I have, all that I am? It surely means that we mustn't take ourselves too seriously, that by not owning the being we are given custody of, we experience that freeing sensation of not having to become one's own center of gravity—like the blessed angels, who, says Chesterton, are free to fly precisely because they take themselves so lightly.

In his delightful book, *The Poet And The Lunatics*, Chesterton writes:

> Man is a creature; all his happiness consists in being a creature; or, as the Great Voice commanded us, in being a child. All his fun is in having a gift or present; which the child values because it is a 'surprise.' But surprise implies that a thing came from outside ourselves; and gratitude that it comes from someone other than ourselves. It is thrust through the letter-box; it is thrown in at the window; it is thrown over the wall. Those limits are the lines of the very plan of human pleasure. [1]

This surely accounts for the fact that, as any decent moral tradition would tell us, the first obligation of the creature is gratitude. We ought to be jolly thankful for a gift which none of us could himself give. There can be very little pleasure in giving yourself a present. But because it is God making me a present of myself, and then, the gift having turned out not to be enough owing to the grief of sin, thereupon making a gift of *Himself*, we exclaim with unwonted delight. Like the little boy in that magical movie, *Life is Beautiful*, who shouts at the very end, his father having made the sacrifice of his life for him, "We won! We won! A thousand points! We get to keep the green tank! Couldn't you just die laughing . . . ?"

Do you know that film? It is unforgettable. A favorite of Pope John Paul II, who pronounced it a masterpiece.

All right. So why am I going on like this? Because God manifested the mystery of Himself and His gracious will only to the childlike, the simple,

---

1. *The Poet and the Lunatics: Episodes in the Life of Gabriel Gale* (Mineola: Courier Dover Publications, 2012), 72.

the pure and transparent ones. Meanwhile, the wise and the clever haven't the capacity to understand a thing, they haven't a clue. Jesus' attitude toward these little ones could hardly be more clear or convicting. Confronted with a child on the street, whom the disciples mobilize at once to keep from Him, as if his proximity to the Lord was like a toxic stain, Jesus rebukes them, saying: "Let the children come to me, and do not hinder them" (Mt 19:14). In other words, suffer these little ones to come unto Christ. Do not come between Christ and the child! Because, says Jesus, "Whoever receives one such child in my name receives me" (Mt 18:5).

In the last year of his life, 1988, before entering into the eternal childhood of God, Hans Urs von Balthasar wrote a stunning little book entitled, *Unless You Become Like This Child*. Less than eighty pages, it is luminous with beauty and insight. A child, he informs us, "is not merely a distant analogy for the Son of God." Turning to such a child in Jesus' name, he insists, is nothing less than "welcoming the archetypical Child who has his abode in the Father's bosom. And because this Child cannot be separated from his abode, whoever turns to the most insignificant of children is, in fact, attaining to the ultimate, to the Father himself." [2] For does not Jesus Himself tell us, "whoever receives me, receives not me but him who sent me" (Mk 9:37)?

This is not an exercise in social welfare, by the way, but, insists Balthasar, a profound mystery, "rooted in the very being of Christ, whose identity is inseparable from his being a child in the bosom of the Father. . . ."[3] That profound and intimate filial connection, lived out from all eternity within the household of God, reveals to us who are privy to its mystery something of the preciousness of every child. It throws light upon the great mystery of childhood, of innocence, "the ways of the child (which), long since sealed off for the adult, open up an original dimension in which everything unfolds within the bounds of the right, the true, the good."[4] Far from being a merely transitional stage—that is, the time spent when the kid is not yet an adult and those who impatiently wish he'd hurry up and get on with it—"that zone or dimension in which the child lives, on the contrary, reveals itself as a sphere of original wholeness and health."[5] It is a privileged period in the unfolding drama of a man's life. It is a time of peculiar, persisting vulnerability as well.

---

2. San Francisco: Ignatius Press, 1991, 10.
3. Ibid., 11.
4. Ibid., 12.
5. Ibid., 12.

How else do we explain the threatening words Jesus hurls at the seducer of the young and the childlike? "It would be better for him if a millstone were hung round his neck and he were cast into the sea, than that he should cause one of these little ones to sin" (Lk 17:2).

Children—and having raised a busload myself I can appreciate the point—believe the stories they are told. They are far likelier to believe, say, in fiery dragons and talking donuts than events accurately set down in the daily press, which tend to be pretty boring and predictable anyway. I can still vividly recall my daughter Francesca, beginning around age three or four, repeatedly asking, "When, Papa, will God open the clouds and come down?" What could I say? "How on earth should I know? I'm only a theologian. Go ask your mother!" Who must have told her because she no longer asks. In fact, she later became a student at the University where I teach . . . studying theology!

As St. Paul famously put it, "Knowledge inflates, love builds up." What is inflated, of course, is very often hollow, void of substance. Like the hot air balloon waiting to be burst, the pomposities of the wise and the clever evince neither humility nor life. They do not edify.

> The endless cycle of idea and action,
> Endless invention, endless experiment,
> Brings knowledge of motion, but not of stillness;
> Knowledge of speech, but not of silence;
> Knowledge of words, and ignorance of the Word.
> All our knowledge brings us nearer to our ignorance,
> All our ignorance brings us nearer to death,
> But nearness to death no nearer to God.
> Where is the Life we have lost in living?
> Where is the wisdom we have lost in knowledge?
> Where is the knowledge we have lost in information?
> The cycles of Heaven in twenty centuries
> Bring us farther from God and nearer to the Dust.
> (T. S. Eliot, "*Choruses from the Rock*")[6]

It is a very long poem, by the way, but near the end, eighteen or so pages later, he concludes with the following summary; it is full of mordant wit:

---

6. From *The Complete Poems*, 96.

> And the wind shall say: 'Here were decent godless people:
> Their only monument the asphalt road
> And a thousand lost golf balls.[7]

There was an eighteenth century clergyman acquaintance of Dr. Johnson, who tended, he said, to unsettle everything without ever settling anything. He is back in the saddle. Alive and well among a good many theologians, too, who appear very wise and clever indeed. But how often they seem determined on unsettling the faith of the simple! And who are the simple? Those whose instincts are compact of faith but who cannot always find the right word with which to disarm the enemies of that faith. Is this why Jesus speaks those frightening words about the millstone tied around the neck of the tempter? Is that why he threatens the "blind leaders" who slam shut the portal leading to paradise? They haven't the least intention of going there themselves, yet they would thwart the simple who appear so blithe and ardent to enter in. How do they do this? By throwing up huge exegetical constructs, scaffolding of the most vast and learned scholarship, in order to intimidate and confound the simple, who evince this great hunger for God's Word, dumbly perceiving its importance to their lives.

To be sure, there are often tensions between the faith of the simple and the erudition of the experts. But even the most naïve piety need not shrink from scientific rigor or curiosity, any more than there need be a disconnect between the realms of grace and nature, revelation and reason, heaven and history. I think of Etienne Gilson's inspired observation about the construction of the great Gothic cathedrals of Northern Europe; a happy combination, he said, of piety and geometry. Where there is opposition, it is most speedily put to rest by a resolute willingness on both sides to see in the witness of Scripture itself a full and credible account of the entirety of the Mystery of Jesus; an account mediated at every turn by holy Church, His Bride and Body. I say that because, while the body of Scripture grows out of the life of the Church, and may not be understood apart from her, her own life and mission spring directly from Christ Himself. Indeed, the bride herself mysteriously emerges from the pierced and stricken side of the crucified God Himself, who hung lifeless and alone upon the Cross for the world's salvation.

---

7. Ibid., 103.

Let us ask our suffering Lord for the grace always to approach the Mystery through the life of the bride, for whose sake He broke His body and shed His blood, thus vouchsafing the twin Sacraments of Baptism and Eucharist. And thus to be grateful for all that He gives us through her.

THE CONCEPTION AND THE CROSS

There exists a charming and instructive tradition in the Church—perhaps of apocryphal origin, I do not know—which traces its pedigree back at least as far as Tertullian, that fiery North African Father of the third century, according to which our Blessed Lord died on the Cross exactly thirty-three years to the day following His conception by the Holy Spirit in the womb of His virgin mother Mary. It all happened on the twenty-fifth of March, the feast of the Lord's Annunciation, one of two feasts on which we are expected to genuflect while reciting the creed. And the other? The Nativity of the Lord—Christmas—falling nine months to the day later.

By means, therefore, of a most extraordinary convergence of calendar dates, which only God Himself would seem clever enough to contrive, both events—Conception and Cross—events on which the world's salvation depends, Mary was there, remaining equally and indispensably present to each. Both at the beginning, when the Word took flesh, and at the very end when that same flesh—blood, marrow, and bone—were nailed to the Cross, His spirit descending into the silence and the horror of Sheol: *She was there*. And the point of all this? I mean, where am I going with this conceit of the calendar? This isn't an exercise in Mariology, but rather a series of conferences on the theme of Christ, so what is my point?

Well, two things, two points need to be made which bear upon that Christological theme, including also the practical fallout for the life of men from it. The first is the fact that all salvation depends on Mary, because it comes through Mary. If the success of her Son's saving mission requires the prior consent of the mother, then it follows that her co-operation is crucial to the plan of God. Maybe that is why the single most important four letter word in the language is *fiat*, even if it isn't an English word. May all this, says Mary in reply to the astonishing invitation issued by the angel, "be done unto me according to *thy* (meaning God's) word." She does not withhold the freedom of her will, but instead surrenders it perfectly to God. And, second, whatever correlative understanding we come to concerning Christ and the redemption He wrought, it must likewise derive from her, from she who became, in the happy phrase coined by the poet Wordsworth, "our tainted nature's solitary boast."[1]

What an amazing conjunction that is! That both the Word whose sudden and unforeseen eruption into our world, and the matchless wisdom to understand the burden Christ came to bear, entirely derive from the Woman whose whole mystery is of a piece with the unseen God of whom, in a daring condescension from on high, she became the ordinary human mother. She who is "younger than sin," to recall a lovely line from Bernanos, became the vessel—the sacred viaduct stretched between earth and sky—across which God Himself poured out the undivided substance of His eternal and triune life into the life of man. Indeed, the very one who, in Augustine's inspired image, "gave milk to our bread." Could there exist among mere mortals a destiny higher than this?

If God breaks Himself to become our bread, then we surely need to know something of the woman whose recipe made possible the production no less of the loaf. Of course, putting it with perfect accuracy, the recipe belongs to God, but to whom did He entrust the work that needed to be done in the kitchen? That's the question. And the point is, it all flows through her. Certainly the event of the incarnate God turns entirely on her willingness to become the human source of the divine river, the human origin of the gift that is nothing less than God Himself. Who else does Jesus look like if not the mother whose body fashioned His own? At the same time, our very understanding, the extent to which we succeed in unpuzzling the Mystery, that too derives entirely from her, the living memory of all that God entrusted to the mother of His Son.

---

1. William Wordsworth, from his poem, "The Virgin," from his *Ecclesiastical Sonnets*. It begins, "Mother! whose virgin bosom was uncrost / With the least shade of thought to sin allied; / Woman! above all women glorified, / our tainted nature's solitary boast."

Balthasar surely has the sense of it when, in writing about faith, he reminds us that it involves the surrender of the entire person to God. "Because Mary from the start surrendered everything, her memory was the unsullied tablet on which the Father, through the Spirit, could write His entire Word." What an astonishing assertion that is. That it is precisely her memory we need to consult in order to learn anything of relevance about Christ. And how wonderfully available to us it now is, thanks to the profundity of her prior surrender. Giving herself totally over to Him, God thus enables her, in a gesture of *kenosis* greater than any in the universe (save only the example of her Son), to pour herself out upon the Church. Here I am reminded of a superb and telling sentence from Gertrude von le Fort: "Surrender to God is the only absolute power that the creature possesses."[2]

Or put it this way, which is how Dante presents the business when, in the final canto of the *Paradiso*, he ascribes a lovely prayer to St. Bernard, to whom he has recourse in obtaining the great object of his desire, namely to see the face of God. And, by the way, for all that it is humanly impossible to look on the face of God and live, the human need to do so, that is, freely to gaze upon the transfigured face of Jesus Christ on whom shines the glory—the *Kabod*—of God Himself, remains the deepest driving desire we possess. Indeed, it possesses us, evincing a persistence greater even than the need for sex, or food, or shelter, or power, or prestige. Here is the prayer placed on his lips by which Dante's entreaty may be answered: "Lady, thou are so great and so powerful that those who desire grace yet will not turn to thee, shall have their desires fly without wings."

What better advocate than she for whose sake, as Dante reminds us, the very Maker of the universe did not disdain to become His own making? Like an elevator, a rocket ship no less, she is the perfect intermediary for all our needs. Her mediation is not merely helpful in the sense of rendering access more easily to God, but that unless one goes through her one simply cannot go to God. She is indispensable, I am saying. The very one, says Augustine, "whom the heavens cannot contain, the womb of one woman bore." Go figure as they say.

The poet Hopkins in lines of riveting lyric intensity taken from his poem, unforgettably named, "The Blessed Mother Compared To The Air We Breathe," has described her as someone who "This one work has to do . . . Let all God's glory through." And all of us, he says, "are meant to share . . . Her life as life does air." The poet's homage to our common mother is wonderfully,

2. Gertrude von le Fort, *The Eternal Woman*, (Milwaukee: The Bruce Publishing Company, 1962), 13.

relentlessly over-the-top, beginning with this opening salvo: "Wild air, world-mothering air, / Nestling me everywhere." Waxing ever more extravagant as he heaps praise upon praise, he continues:

> This needful, never spent,
> And nursing element
> My more than meat and drink,
> My meal at every wink;
> This air, which, by life's law,
> My lung must draw and draw
> Now but to breathe its praise,
> Minds me in many ways
> Of her who not only
> Gave God's infinity
> Dwindled to infancy
> Welcome in womb and breast,
> Birth, milk, and all the rest
> But mothers each new grace
> That does now reach our race—

How hard it is, once started on line after line of this superbly sacramental artist, to simply cease and desist. Let me conclude, then, with a few more samples of Mary's unique mediation in the order of grace, of that salvation of which she is the supreme midwife.

> I say that we are wound
> With mercy round and round
> As if with air . . .
>
> And men are meant to share
> Her life as life does air.
> If I have understood
> She holds high motherhood
> Towards all our ghostly good
> And plays in grace her part
> About man's beating heart,

Laying, like air's fine flood,
The death dance in his blood . . .
And makes, O marvelous!
New Nazareths in us,
Where she shall yet conceive
Him, morning, noon, and eve.

It is, unassailably, art of the first intensity; both gorgeous in its imagery and profound in its grasp of the central fact of faith, that Christ, who is ever present, comes irrepressibly into our world and our lives precisely through the flesh of His mother, who is our mother too.

O Mary, you embody / All God taught to our race, / For you are first and foremost / In fullness of his grace; / We praise this wondrous honor / That you gave birth to him / Who from you took his manhood /
And saved us from our sin.

Liturgy of the Hours
Feast of the Visitation

AT THE STILL POINT OF
THE TURNING WORLD

Suppose we begin with this sundering question, and see if we can't pin it to the floor. What is the thing that finally defines the difference between Christianity and every other competing creed in the universe? Only we mustn't call it a thing, as if the Christian Story were like an episode in a TV series, whose theme and plot appear as nearly interchangeable as any other; or like a piece of wood you might inventory in a lumber yard.

What I'm asking, then, is whether or not there exists an essential and defining point of disagreement, of division, between the Christian religion and everything else? Is there a place where the distinctively Christian absolutely diverges, moving in a direction totally outside and beyond anything and everything else on the planet? A moment, say, when a fellow like Plato, whom you've invited for coffee and donuts, goes absolutely ballistic, and runs screaming from the room? A moment, in short, when this ancient architect of idealism cannot abide the cuisine, indeed, would sooner rend his garments than submit to the menu that marks your faith?

Give up? It is the Incarnation. That wholly and everlastingly shocking event of the enfleshment of God. The scandal of particularity. If it be thought odd of God to choose the Jew, how infinitely more odd that God should Himself become a Jew? And where and when does it all happen? "At the still point of the turning world," says Eliot,

> Where past and future are gathered.
> . . . Except for the point, the still point,
> There would be no dance and there is only the dance.
> (T. S. Eliot, "Burnt Norton")[1]

That is where Christianity uniquely begins. *HIC VERBUM CARO FACTUM EST. AND THE WORD WAS MADE FLESH AND DWELT AMONG US.* God pitching His tent in the midst of men. Incredible. Dante's description, lifted from the pages of the *Paradiso*, perfectly captures what has happened. "Where every where and every when is focused"—he tells us. But where and when might that be? Is it possible to precise? It is. You have only to zero in on a tiny, unsuspecting, jerkwater town called Nazareth on the twenty-fifth of March in the year AD 1. "The hint half-guessed," writes Eliot, "the gift half-understood, is Incarnation.

> Here the impossible union
> Of spheres of existence is actual,
> Here the past and future
> Are conquered and reconciled.
> ("The Dry Salvages")[2]

And even if, as he tells us in that marvelous penitential poem called "Ash Wednesday,"

> . . . the lost word is lost, if the spent word is spent
> If the unheard, unspoken
> Word is unspoken, unheard;
> Still is the unspoken word, the Word unheard,
> The Word without a word, the Word within
> The world and for the world;
> And the light shone in darkness and

---

1. First of Eliot's *Four Quartets*, 119.
2. Third of *Four Quartets*, 136.

Against the Word the unstilled world still whirled
About the centre of the silent Word.[3]

How can that be? Because it is nothing less than God's own Word, God's definitive deed, into which all that is God, the totality of the reality we call God, is poured out, spoken finally and unrepeatably into our world. Beginning in time, bisecting the whole order of time, of what we call history, Christ's coming among us breaks ground in an absolutely new and fresh and radically comprehensive way. "He brought all newness in bringing himself," reports the sainted bishop and martyr Irenaeus. "Here," pronounces Pope John Paul II in his *Letter* preparing the world for the great Jubilee of the year 2000, "is the starting point. . . . Here, it is not simply a case of man seeking God, but of God who comes in Person to speak to man of himself and to show him the path by which he may be reached."[4]

Please note what is going on here. To begin with, there is the whole annihilating distinction between religion, which is natural to man, and Revelation, of which only God can be the catalyst; between, that is, the upward thrust of man in search of God—sensitive therefore to all the vibrations of the transcendent—and God's own answering response in the cruciform shape of the Son who comes in search of man. Indeed, who descends to the very depth of man's disaffection from God, his desolation endured in the absence of God. And what is it all for? Only this: to show us the face of God, the absolute paternal presence that will never forsake us; and to show us precisely how to find the true way home to the Father.

"God goes in search of man," the pope reminds us. "Jesus speaks of this search as the finding of a lost sheep (cf. Lk 15:1–7).[5] It is a search which begins in the heart of God and culminates in the Incarnation of the Word." And why should God wish to go in search of man? Because God who is *Love* has chosen, out of an incomprehensible depth of love, to show this love to the world, in order to raise man to a level of unheard of intimacy with Himself. "He loved them to the last," the Gospel of John tells us.

Nowhere, it seems to me, is that encounter rendered with greater profundity than in the story of the Pilgrim-Poet Dante, whose moving description in the final section of *The Divine Comedy*, perhaps the greatest poetic achievement

---

3. *The Complete Poems*, 65.
4. *Tertio Millennio Adveniente* (November 10, 1994), no. 6.
5. Ibid., no. 7.

this side of Sacred Scripture, carries him right to the heart of God. What does Dante see? Looking into the heart of the Triune God, whom does he see?

Well, I'm not about to tell you. At least not until you've learned two things. How far Dante has come. And on whose wings he is enabled to fly so high. Which, in order to answer, requires that we return once more to the first page of the first book where, lost in the Dark Wood on the afternoon of Good Friday in the year 1300, we find him in the very middle of the journey of his life. Having lost his way, beset on every side by fear, temptation and sin, the poor man simply does not know where to turn. And so, in the grip of sudden, overpowering panic, he cries out, desperate to escape so enveloping a sense of being lost. What else can he do but externalize his fear? Who among us has not been in the same predicament, has not felt the same terror? It is the sudden, paralyzing sense that not only am I lost, but that I might never be found. One is face to face with pure, primal fear. It is to force a man out into an extremity of isolation and loss that none of us were created to have to endure. Only God can reach that far into the soul of my wretchedness and pry me loose. Only He can dismantle brick by brick, as it were, the walls that enclose the person trapped inside the cell of one's own self. "The lost are like this," cries out the poet Hopkins in one of those "terrible sonnets," that evoke with bitter eloquence the felt absence of God's presence. Only, he adds, "their scourge to be / As I am mine, their sweating selves; but worse."[6]

And in the case of Dante, all at once, like a lightning flash, the figure of Our Lady intervenes, prompted by the prayers of his beloved Beatrice, and all the saints in heaven, most especially Bernard of Clairvaux, who along with all the blessed spirits conspire to set him free from the Dark Wood, the self-imposed prison in which he lives.

It is the final canto of the poem, the concluding phase of the journey, in which Dante is to be at last lifted onto the plane of heavenly glory. There at the threshold awaiting the ministrations of the Holy Virgin, Dante acknowledges the homage paid her by St. Bernard, who pronounces her "humble beyond all creatures and more exalted," the sheer weight of whose worth "so ennobled human nature / that its divine Creator did not scorn / to make Himself the creature of His creature." Indeed, she is so great and has such power "that

---

6. Gerard Manley Hopkins, from "I Wake and Feel the Fell of Dark, Not Day" from *A Hopkins Reader* (New York: Doubleday/Image, 1966), 77.

who seeks grace and does not first seek thee / would have his wish fly upward without wings."

Who can imagine such a thing? Yet, Bernard tells us, she is so gracious that often she will assist us far in advance of our asking, anticipating the need even before it has risen to the level of prayer. And since the desire Dante has is nothing less than to enter into the Precincts of Eternal Felicity, he will need no little assistance from her.

She does not disappoint, either. As her child, her special charge, annealed to her heart, Dante is at once transported to the inner life of God.

> Within the depthless deep and clear existence
> of that abyss of light three circles shown—
> three in color, one in circumference:
> the second from the first, rainbow from rainbow;
> the third, an exhalation of pure fire
> equally breathed forth by the other two.

"O how my speech falls short," he exclaims, the resources of language suddenly shattered and spent before the awful immensity of God. "And for what I can see," he adds, "It is not enough to say that I say little."

Poor Dante. It is not his fault that the best he can manage is a mere lifeless geometric figure to represent the unspeakability of the Tri-Une God. But he has certainly done his best, which is good enough to qualify the book as among the enduring masterpieces of world literature.

However, there is yet more to it. For within the bright nimbus of Light shining eternally forth from the three circles of which the poet speaks, something entirely new and unforeseen and unimaginable emerges to rivet absolutely the attention of the pilgrim-poet. It is the human face of Jesus, God's own Word become flesh, that now appears so startlingly stark and vivid before the baffled gaze of Dante, so utterly stunned and stupefied by a sight he had not expected to see. So blown away is he by the Image, this sudden visual sighting of a God "painted with our effigy," that Dante compares himself to a "geometer who sets himself / to square the circle, and is unable to think / of the formula to solve the problem."

He thereupon falls into a state of rhapsodic wonder, a tremor of bliss before the face of his own likeness. It is the greatest possible discovery a man could make; greater even than that of fire at the dawn of time. For here is the fire of Divine Love revealed in the face of Christ, whose human countenance may now be found at the heart and center of both God and man. In Christ we are invited to see, all at once, both the closeness of God before the world He made and the promise of man standing entirely re-made before the God who loved him to the end.

> So was I faced with this new vision:
> I wanted to see how the image could fit the circle
> and how it could be that that was where it was . . .

Alas, even the high imagination ("*alta fantasia*") of Dante, fails at this point ("not a flight for my wings," he laments), leaving him however with the blinding affirmation that is the cornerstone of the Christian faith. "*And the Word was made flesh and dwelt among us.*"

GOD IS LOVE

Imagine Sacred Scripture as one vast and varied library of Spirit inspired literature. Now picture two bookends between which this immense narrative unfolds. Have you got that? In the drama of God's relationship with the world, two fixed points define and determine everything else. The whole shooting match, in short, compressed between two ends, two flash points lighting up the entire night sky of divine Revelation.

What are these benchmarks? And why are they so climactic to an understanding of the story Scripture tells us? Because, very simply, they represent the highpoints of both Old and New Testament theology, the acme of all that God aims to impart about Himself and about the world He made and then, under the stress of human sin and stupidity, re-made. Namely, that He exists (point one), and that His existence (point two) is nothing other than eternal, unending Love.

One might even put it epigrammatically, saying—Yes, God is. And, yes, this very *is-ing* that is God is nothing other than the fact that the God who is, is Love. That He manifests this Being-Who-Is-Love from all eternity from within the perfect life of the Blessed Trinity; and that when He chose to manifest this same truth about Himself on the outside, He created the world into which

He then inserted Himself. ("The historical self-emptying of the eternal self-interpretation of the Father in the Son," is how Veronica Donnelly put it in her superb study of Balthasar, entitled *Saving Beauty: Form As the Key to Balthasar's Christology*, 2007, p. 252.) How amazingly He has filled it, too, including so many impossible people like you and me.

Where do these discoveries come from? If they did not simply fall out of the sky, is there evidence of these two bookends, say, from Scripture itself? There is and it is unassailable. The first is clearly signposted in the Book of Exodus, chapter three, where Moses, accosted by the Voice summoning him to the Burning Bush, dares to ask, "Who are you?" And God obligingly answers the upstart Hebrew in a voice of thunder: "*I AM WHO AM!*" Then there is the famous passage from the fourth chapter of the First Letter of John, where, beginning with verse seven, we are enjoined to love one another, "for love is of God, and he who loves is born of God and knows God," and that "He who does not love does not know God; *for God is love.*"

Taken together, I want to suggest, these two landmark texts—living monuments to the faith of Israel and the Church—constitute the entire bedrock belief we have that unless God is, and unless He is love—to strike the sheer interchangeability of being and love, existence and *eros*—our condition remains entirely hopeless. Forever. No exit from the hell of human hopelessness.

Why is that? Because only a God who exists as pure unchanging love would dare to undertake so madly improbable a descent into the muck and the mire of a fallen and depraved world. And why would God want to do that? Because He is love and because He loves us. In order precisely to set us free from the hellish torment of sin and death, I am saying, God elected to enter even into the depths of that hell to which our lives would otherwise be forced to submit.

How beautifully the late pope has illustrated all this in that remarkable book he wrote back in 1994, almost ten years before his death, *Crossing the Threshold of Hope*, wherein he wrestles with hard questions put to him by a tough examiner. Why is there so much evil and suffering in the world? Must God put up with it? Was it really necessary to suffer the Son to hang upon the Cross? Couldn't the world's salvation come any cheaper?

These are not puff balls easily deflected by anyone. Indeed, they take us all by the throat, including God's Vicar. Why couldn't God have justified Himself before the world, whose judgments are replete with evidence of the world's wickedness, without having to go up to Golgotha in the first place? Was it really necessary, the pope is asking, to place Christ's Cross at the center of that history? After all, God in His omnipotence—the *Pantokrator*, no less, of the planet—can do pretty much anything He pleases. Why couldn't He just tell the world to go stuff it?

The pope's answer is irrefutably eloquent. Because God, he reminds us, who is infinitely more than mere omnipotence, actually wants to justify Himself to the world He made. Imagine that. He does not wish to impose a solution upon the world. Instead He invited us to consider the proposal He makes, even as it qualifies as one no greater than which any man can imagine. "He is not the Absolute that remains outside of the world, indifferent to human suffering. He is *Emmanuel*, God-with-us, a God who shares man's lot and participates in his destiny."[1]

Isn't this the fatal flaw that brings down the religion of Islam, that its God stands essentially outside the world, the letters of whose Name could never spell *Emmanuel*? "Some of the most beautiful names in the human language are given to the God of the Koran, but he is ultimately a God outside of the world, a God who is only Majesty, never *Emmanuel*, God-with-us. Islam," the pope tells us, "is not a religion of redemption."[2]

It is because God is always to be found with those who suffer, always in solidarity with the least and the lost and the unlovely, that Christianity continues to commend itself to the poor and dispossessed. And, yet, He could so easily have circumvented the Cross, had He wished to do so (in fact, it was mockingly proposed to Him as He hung there in agony), and still have saved the world. He is God, for heaven sakes! But He did not. "The fact that he stayed on the Cross until the end, the fact that on the Cross he could say, as do all who suffer: 'My God, my God, why have you forsaken me?' (Mk 15:34), has remained in human history the strongest argument. If the agony of the Cross had not happened," the pope daringly concludes, "the truth that God is Love would have been unfounded."[3]

What else have broken spirits and diseased bodies to count on if not a God the very design of whose being is determined always on their behalf? But for the God who is love through and through, the world would perish for want of hope, falling headlong and forever into hell. Who, save the God of love alone, could accept responsibility for the world's dereliction? In a stunning essay by

---

1. Pope John Paul II, *Crossing the Threshold of Hope* (New York: Knopf, 1995), from his chapter, "Why Is There So Much Suffering In The World?" beginning on p. 60.
2. Ibid., chapter entitled "Muhammad?" 92.
3. Ibid., chapter entitled "Why Does God Tolerate Suffering?" 66.

Balthasar entitled *"Only If,"* the celebrated Swiss theologian asks the question that only a theology grounded in a God who is love can answer, indeed, can succeed in assuaging the countless losses sustained in a fallen world. Who will redeem, he asks, "the unthinkable sufferings and despair, the senseless, horrible destruction of beings whose purpose for existence had to be contained in the narrow circle of birth and death?"[4]

Surely no God of mere power would wish to shoulder responsibility for the endless impacted miseries of His work. At most He might offer Himself as that state of forgetful sleep on the far side of human suffering, the peace no less of the grave. But no amnesiac answer to our insupportably painful existence will do. And, to be sure, God would never as all-powerful Creator alone have consented really to do more, that is, to endure the pain and the grief of complete godforsakenness so that, from within, it might stand redeemed. Who, then, to take up Balthasar's insistent question, will gather up the futilities and despairs?

> Who has so much compassion that he does not simply watch sympathetically (from his own freedom from suffering which he perhaps has achieved), nor wrathfully plan for redress (for the next time), but in solidarity bears the responsibility for all that cries to heaven, bears it in compassion (which must cry ever more frightfully to heaven)? . . . only if this one not only shares in the most terrible anguish but surpasses it by laying hold of it from below (for only God can know what it means to be truly forsaken by God), only if that Maximum coincides with this Minimum (both beyond our comprehension)—not in indifference, but in such a way that absolute power becomes one with absolute powerlessness in sheltering compassion . . .[5]

In the parable of the Prodigal Son, he comments, there is one figure whose presence is strangely absent from the story, namely the narrator, who is Christ, the very image and likeness of the Father's love. Who, says Balthasar, "goes silently along the way into complete abandonment—suffering with us, truly

4. From his book *Convergences: To the Source of Christian Mystery* (San Francisco: Ignatius Press, 1983), 135–153.
5. Ibid., 136–137.

representing all of us." Thus, the Father not only waits for the Prodigal to come home on his own,

> but (in the form of his son) sends out his love into his desolation. He allows his son to identify himself with his lost brother. And by this very power of identifying himself—without keeping a respectable distance—with his complete opposite, God the Father recognized the consubstantiality, the divinity of the one he has sent as his redeeming word into the world.[6]

How clearly we now see the determination of God to render absolutely, dramatically credible to the creature, the whole inner truth of the Word's enfleshment in human life and history. Having entered entirely into the brokenness of our condition, God evinces total and perfect passion for all human pain and loss. Eliot's image of the "wounded surgeon" provides an almost perfect metaphor for the redemption wrought by the Son of God.

> The wounded surgeon plies the steel
> That questions the distempered part;
> Beneath the bleeding hands we feel
> The sharp compassion of the healer's art
> Resolving the enigma of the fever chart.[7]

Let us turn then to so adroit and loving a Divine Physician; who not only restores the soul to health, but does so in so sublimely paradoxical a way as to take on the very disease He has promised to deliver us from.

---

6. See my book, *The Suffering of Love: Christ's Descent Into the Hell of Human Hopelessness* (Petersham MA: St. Bede's Publications, 1995), 79.
7. From "East Coker," second of *Four Quartets* by T. S. Eliot from *The Complete Poems*, 127.

THE SUFFERING OF LOVE

It was a number of years ago that St. Bede's Press brought out my first book, *The Suffering Of Love*, based on a dissertation I had done in Rome while a student at the Angelicum. The years spent in Rome were wholly delightful, by the way. The publishing house is no longer standing, but the book has managed to survive, although sales have never been brisk. (The story, alas, of all my books. Their shelf-life, I often tell friends, is a bit like yogurt.) However, Ignatius Press having recently re-issued the thing, including a splendid new cover, I expect an avalanche of royalties will soon follow.

The title of the book is based on a line from Origen, among the greatest of the Church Fathers, who, in asking about the nature of the suffering of God, answers very simply that it was the suffering of love. "First he suffered, then he came down. . . ." In other words, from all eternity there persists this mysterious *pathos* inscribed in the very heart of God, encompassing the whole life of the *Logos*, and that it is nothing less than *a suffering of love*.

In setting out to defend that particular thesis, I found myself writing at length about the anguish of human suffering, especially as regards the awful ordeal of the Jewish people, whose torments have coincided with its long and troubled history. And, of course, at the heart of the suffering inflicted upon this peculiar People of the Promise (How odd of God to choose the Jew!), is the question that has haunted all of Judaism: Where was God during the time of the Nazi Holocaust? When the cry of His people went unheard amid the Death Camps of the Third Reich—what was God doing? Why did He not intervene, put a stop to the slaughter of so many millions of His children?

It is a question not only applicable to the Jews, as if they alone were victims of an insane ideology, but to everyone whose lives have been blasted by evil and injustice. A recent book I came across has recounted in fairly harrowing detail the fate of thousands of non-Jews who perished at Dachau, a notorious Nazi killing field. Their crime? They were all Roman Catholic priests and therefore presumptive enemies of the Aryan State.

Where in fact is God to be found in any of the myriad horrors of apparent meaningless misery that mark the long dark journey of our fallen human history? Where is God in the midst of one's own pain? It is not a question any of us, it seems to me, is at liberty not to ask. Because the whole weight and outcome of our faith, no less, depends on the answer to that question. God, too, is implicated in this business, which is the whole theme of theodicy. There has simply got to be an answer to the problem of pain if the justice and holiness of God are to be vindicated in the face of evil. Classically understood, the problem is this: If God is really good, and if His omnipotence is equal to that goodness, then surely He would both wish to rid the world of evil, and He would additionally possess the capacity to do so. Yet the flames of evil and injustice persist in devouring the good and the innocent. So perhaps God is neither all-good nor all-powerful. Neat, isn't it?

And so, at one stroke, the whole Christian conception of God self-destructs, vaporized by the force of the polemic thrown up against God.

The stakes are enormous, incalculable even. So how does Christianity respond to what appears to be an absolutely crushing claim? What is the proposal of faith that, in the teeth of all the arguments thrown up against God, actually vanquishes the enemy? It is the fact of Jesus Christ. Most especially in the event of His Cross, followed by the terrifying descent into hell, the extreme limit of the *kenosis* of God. Only then will the hell of human hopelessness find an absolute and ultimate deliverance from the absurdity of sin and death.

There is real kinship here, between the experience of Christ's own abandonment, hellishly borne on the Cross, and then into the desolation of Holy Saturday, and all the accumulated agony of human suffering and loss in the world and its history. A depth of kinship and solidarity so radical that it reaches right down to the very bottom of our wounded being, in order to restore and set right the whole human predicament. Sheer, incomprehensible kinship in *kenosis*.

"Look Lord," exclaims that marvelous Elizabethan poet John Donne, "and find both Adams met in me; / As the first Adam's sweat surrounds my face, / May the last Adam's blood my soul embrace."[1] Christ, you see, becomes the mediating figure between Jew and Christian, between you and me. If man is the middle term, as Pascal tells us, between nothing and everything, then Christ, the perfect Man, has come to occupy that space, filling it with Himself.

Or this rhapsodic burst from Gerard Manley Hopkins, exhorting us to see how in God's eye we are all one in Christ: ". . . for Christ plays in ten thousand places, / Lovely in limbs and lovely in eyes not his / To the Father through the features of men's faces."[2]

Where else in this world are we to find the "still point" that does not move, "the point of intersection," on whose axis all the converging forces meet? It is that sacred site where the sin and suffering of man meet the justice and holiness of God. It is the absolute center of Christian faith and theology, without which we are nothing. In fact, we are less than zero. "Man without grace," Eric Voegelin has said, "is demonic nothingness."

And just as Christology stands at the center, the saving presence of Christ ascending to the very summit of the stair—the Word who was in the beginning and without whom there could not be any beginning—so too does it possess it own center, which is the Cross, on which the atoning event of His death took place. To that "still point" everything else in the universe is directed, whether it be Christ's own life, whose natural trajectory draws Him inexorably to death, or our own lives, whose point of balance and finality derive from Christ.

Seeing the whole sweep of things from that perspective, it becomes clear that life is best understood as a movement, a coursing, from beginning to end, first to last, crib to cross. From the self-emptying of God into the womb of the woman, His Virgin Mother; to the crib in Bethlehem; to the nursery and workbench of Nazareth; to the wood of the Cross on Calvary; to the crypt of Holy Saturday. So it goes: the slow, protracted torture and death of God-as-man; from which the world derives its salvation and may yet grow into the fullness of Christian discipleship. Out of death comes life. The sheer

1. From his poem entitled "Hymn To God, My God, In My Sickness."
2. From his poem entitled, "As King Fishers Catch Fire."

absoluteness of God bespeaking an Otherness that is unsurpassed by anything in the universe, joined to the majesty of a self-revealing love shown in the life of Jesus. Where else would we be expected to find the high point, if not in the bloody details of his Paschal Mystery? Here is the place where absolute power is made perfect in abject weakness, the glory and splendor of the Lord revealed in the squalor and grief of the Crucified God. Majesty in misery, wealth disguised as poverty, beauty amid ugliness, the immensity of God nailed to the ignominy of the Cross—the list of antitheses leave one breathless before a God entirely defined by paradox.

"See how I make all things new," He tells His mother after falling prostrate to the ground for the third and final time, to recall the terrible beauty of the Mel Gibson movie. It is the decisive "hour," so John the Divine, the beloved apostle, tells us in the Last Gospel, the hour towards which everything in the life of Christ may be said to move in solemn, rhythmic cadence; the awful hour of the Passion when the mission of the *Kyrios* reaches its high point, the most pure and luminous expression of divine self-empting love for the world. "He loved them to the last, to the very end," to sound the clarion call of the Johannine witness.

God, we need constantly to remind ourselves, is always on the side of those who suffer. What else does it mean to speak of Him as love if not to insist that, at the very bottom of His indefectible and unchangeable being, He evince this infinite capacity to suffer with and in and for others? A God who cannot do this, cannot extend Himself in this way, is worse than any wretched being He permits to exist, for they at least can laugh and weep and love. He is no better, it would seem, than the god of Aristotle, the Unmoved Mover whom no one is moved to love. Man may admire His perfected beauty, fear and tremble before His power, but in the end so loveless a being is more bereft than any potsherd of a man who suffers because, at least, he knows how to love.

"Love anything, even a dog," C.S. Lewis warns, "and it will eventually break your heart."[3] A God who cannot love, not because He chooses not to but because being love is simply not constitutive of who God is, is a God constrained by all that He is not to leave His creation utterly vanquished and alone. And it was just this very rejection, set out so emphatically in the Christian creeds, that broke the Aristotelian hold on the doctrine of God. When we insist on the highest scriptural warrant in calling God love, then it follows that He is also

3. Cited by Josef Pieper in his book, *About Love* (Chicago: Franciscan Herald Press, 1974), 76.

a Lover who suffers, whose *Pathos* reveals itself precisely to the extent that He does suffer, daring to descend even into all that is not God, in order thus to redeem and restore the lost and prodigal children of His Father. Not, heaven knows, out of any weakness or imperfection of being, which is why we of course must suffer, but due to the very plenitude—the *Pleroma*—of His being God.

"God comes to pass for man through men," Joseph Ratzinger tells us, "nay, even more concretely, through the man in whom the quintessence of humanity appears and who for that very reason is at the same time God himself. . . . Can we cling at all to the straw of one single historical event? Can we dare to base our whole existence, indeed the whole of history, on the straw of one happening in the great sea of history?"[4] If we cannot do this, if our resistance to what, in an inspired formulation, he has called "the absolutely staggering alliance of *logos* and *sarx* [word and flesh], of meaning and a single historical figure," proves undeniable, then our prospects are very poor and bleak indeed. For a God who is not love will never assume, much less redeem, the world's dereliction; He will instead leave us alone and lost forever.

Let us call upon the God of love, the Eternal Lover, who lost Himself in hell so that we who deserve to go there might find ourselves once more along the high road that leads the fallen human family home to heaven.

---

4. *Introduction to Christianity*, 1969 edition, 142.

"EVEN IF YOU KILL ME, I WILL HAVE HOPE IN YOU"

I can still remember with the most awful sense of dismay, a course I took in graduate school on the Epistles of St. Paul. It was so bone crushingly boring that it nearly killed my appetite for Holy Scripture. So dreadful were my professor's dissections of the Pauline corpus, in fact, that by the time he was through there wasn't much left of the inspired Word of God that he hadn't reduced to ruins. What, I kept asking myself, had become of the sheer dazzling beauty and majesty of the glory of the Lord?

But every so often one stumbles upon a wonderful antidote to the erudite idiocies of much modern Scripture scholarship. For instance, this little book called *The Victory Of Love*, which is nothing less than a profound and beautiful meditation on Chapter Eight of St. Paul's Letter to the Romans. Written by Adrienne von Speyr, a Swiss-Austrian mystic whom Hans Urs von Balthasar received into the Church and would later collaborate with in bringing countless spiritual works to life, her book is a total rehabilitation of the Word of God. It demonstrates the triumph, no less, of the love and the truth that became concretely incarnate in Jesus Christ. All creation is destined to find its ultimate freedom and finality in Christ, whom we are to encounter in the Church who is His Bride and whose ordinary sacramental life is designed to make saints of men.

But what a tiny little book it is! At around one-hundred or so pages, it can hardly compete with tomes whose exegetical throw-weight is often four and five times as much. Ah, but for the sheer wisdom and luminosity distilled in her few pages, it carries more weight than the whole world. She manages to identify what is really the deepest and most abiding attitude of Christ—of the Christ of St. Paul certainly—which is His desire that everyone, "even the last human being in the basket of creation" (what a lovely phrase that is), that even the least prepossessing person on the planet, be saved and thus come to know the surpassing love of God.

> When Paul speaks of the elect he means definite individuals. He sees before his eyes the image of the disciples who followed the Lord . . . the central light falls on them. That this light falls from them on to others, is brought by them to others, is a new truth not excluded but included in the first. . . . The number itself is the Son's secret. It could be that the Father means "many" and that, to speak in a human way, he allows himself to be surprised by the work of the Son who demands "all": Little Thérèse "chose all" when she was offered a basketful of things to choose from. She chose not only what was beautiful but also the unattractive. Thérèse is only imitating what is the deepest in the attitude of the Son of Man: he was the first "to choose all," even the last human being in the basket of creation, perhaps unrecognizable because of sin, but beautiful because the Father created him.[1]

So God, it seems, is determined mightily to move heaven and earth in order to effect our salvation. Because the Father made us out of nothing; because the Son set about re-making us in the frightful Event of His Passion; and because, finally, the Spirit longs to breathe on us in the Pentecostal fire. How else are we to become saints? But the point is, we must not try and fix prematurely the limits of the mercy of God; they are, quite literally, without limit.

Well, then, how does one square any of this with justice, with an all-powerful God giving each man his due? Isn't justice an attribute, among other perfections, that we rightly predicate of God? Isn't the justice of God absolute,

---

1. Adrienne von Speyr, *The Victory of Love* (San Francisco: Ignatius Press, 1990), 8.

pure and unremitting? If the most rigorous and strict application of justice requires that each of us be given exactly what we deserve, then what is to become of the thoroughly wicked, those whose motives are purely malicious and who have, moreover, no interest in reconciling with anyone, certainly not with their victims? Surely any across-the-board application of mercy (in all cases) would amount to a clear and promiscuous perversion of justice. Yes, even if God Himself were to dispense it.

Putting the problem another way, how can God vindicate the innocent without at the same time punishing the guilty? Especially when it is the innocent whom they torment? In short, how are we to square Justice and Mercy? The one consisting of people getting exactly what they deserve; the other determined on not dispensing what they deserve, but the very thing they do not deserve, that is, mercy and forgiveness and love. A colleague of mine, in dealing with students, has put it memorably: Those who come to class, he tells them on the first day, may get mercy. Those who do not, shall get justice. (Note well the asymmetry here: mercy is not certain since it could go the other way, thus expressing its contingent character, that is, its status as purely subjunctive. On the other hand, the certainty of justice, given its grounding in the imperative, permits no escape for the slacker.)

St. Bernard of Clairvaux, in a wonderful sermon, has called these "the two feet of God," warning the sinner to take care lest he neglect both since, "to kiss one without the other is of no avail."[2] What he seems to be saying is that when one is fixated upon, say, justice, one is easily driven to despair since it is not possible for any man perfectly to satisfy the demands of the Law. But if one's fixation is entirely upon mercy, then the resulting fall into presumption will prove fatal. How to reconcile the two, finding the balance between the excesses of each, that is the challenge.

In the *Summa*, St. Thomas has a whole section on this, which he develops on the basis of a single sentence found in St. Anselm. His resolution seems, at one stroke, to solve the whole problem. St. Anselm writes: "If you (O God) punish the wicked it is because of the evil that they do (indeed, I would add, the evil that they in large measure have become, thus their damnation will consist of a suffering entirely self-inflicted). But if you spare them then you are likewise being just because that corresponds to your goodness."

---

2. Sermon 6 on the Song of Songs.

In accosting this statement from Anselm, Thomas argues that between the evil of sinners and the goodness of God, there is simply no equilibrium, no proportionality or balance; that justice is always subordinate to mercy, that it becomes, indeed, a function of mercy, a mode and expression of mercy. So what does that mean? Well, think of it this way. In considering the cosmos, and all the creatures that dwell in it, to what does all that blooming being owe its existence? Can it seriously be the result of God's justice? Surely not since being alive is scarcely what any of us deserve. Does God owe us the title deed on existence? Hardly. On the one hand, He is not constrained by any sort of iron necessity to create any potty little creatures; and, on the other, since none of us may possess himself, how else do we account for our being if not by virtue of having first received it? My life, and the life of the cosmos, must therefore be something God bestows out of His own goodness, love, and freedom. Otherwise it would not be gratuitous and God could not then turn to us in love, in generosity.

So how do we split the difference here; mediate the tension? The answer is hope. The exercise of the virtue of hope collapses all the tension, all the antitheses that threaten the unity struck between justice and mercy. So that in the end, in the mind of God, all the polarities have been surpassed, leaving mercy and justice to join hands, as it were, each of a piece with the other.

I think at once of two extraordinary figures, their witness to an almost limitless horizon of hope the defining feature of their lives. Dame Julian of Norwich, an astonishing woman who lived in the fourteenth century, beneficiary of a series of shattering revelations (she called them *Shewings*) that pushed the envelope of divine solidarity very far indeed. Yet, in transcribing the words of Christ, she is really putting it as God Himself would have us believe. "God is everything that is good," He tells her, "and God has made everything that is made, and God loves everything that he has made. . . . For in mankind, which will be saved, is comprehended all, that is, all that is made and the maker of all; for God is in man, and so in man is all." Amazing! Ah, but Christ is not quite through telling her the extent of the Father's solicitude. "As I have made good the greatest damages," He promises her, "so I intend that you understand from this that I will make good all that is defective."[3]

What kind of God could get away with saying something like that? What must the God of Jesus Christ be like to sustain so sweeping and absolute a

---

3. Cited by Hans Urs von Balthasar in *Dare We Hope That All Men Be Saved?* (San Francisco: Ignatius Press, 1988), 101–102.

hope? "That all shall be well and all manner of thing shall be well." Who can believe it?

How about little Thérèse of Lisieux, then, who believed every word of it? Has the theme of hope ever before found so profound, so perfect an expression? This newest doctor of the Church, who, dying a consumptive at age twenty-four without ever having left the fastness of Carmel, wished to offer her very soul to God, not as a sacrifice to His justice, but precisely to His mercy that knows no limit whatsoever. "If your justice feels inclined to discharge itself," she tells God, "that which, after all, extends only over the earth, how much more, then, does your merciful love yearn to inflame souls, because your mercy, after all, ascends all the way up to heaven." Here is the true audacity of Christian hope, providing the clearest and most consoling evidence of an unbounded trust in the goodness of God. "I believe," she tells us, referring to God and His angels and saints, "that they are waiting to see how far I will go in my trust, but not in vain was my heart pierced by that saying of Job's: 'Even if you kill me, I will have hope in you'."[4]

There is the ground of Christian hope and desire that overcomes the natural (and even supernatural!) fear we all have that, at the end of the day, our sins will keep us from going home to Him. So let us, then, believe and trust in the truth of what she says: "We can never have too much trust in our dear God, who is so powerful and merciful. One receives as much from him as one hopes."[5]

May all our hopes be equal to Him, who loves us more ardently even than we seem to love our sins.

---

4. Ibid., 102–103.
5. Ibid., 103.

HOPE SPRINGS ETERNAL

I have never seriously been tempted to follow the monkish habit of leaping gleefully out of bed at three in the morning. Not once this blessed week, in fact, for all the charms of your company, the godliness of your example, have I been remotely tempted to succumb. As Oscar Wilde would say when temptation struck: "I simply lie down until I get over it." I am, of course, dismayingly familiar with those slackers and slugs who, like myself, dread the coming of the day. We positively recoil at the prospect of having to hit the pavement running. Eagerness in running the race for God, we like to think, is something that can prudently wait until after breakfast; say, around nine or ten in the morning. For us—that is, the mediocre, about whom it has been wittily said that they are always at their best—the real moment of heroism comes when the alarm sounds and we do not at once push the snooze button. We screw up our courage to face the day. "When you awaken with reluctance each morning," Marcus Aurelius reports, "you are not to repine, for you are about to begin the work of a human being."

Now that is very good advice, even when it's being dispensed by a pagan emperor who, when he wasn't writing copybook maxims on the moral life, was pretty busy butchering innocent Christians. I say that because the future belongs to those who show up. It belongs to those unafraid to venture everything they have in terms of an end, a *telos*, towards which they move in a relentless, rhythmic dance. We all need that horizon of absolute fulfillment, the insistent desire and longing that urges us closer and closer to the promised consummation. It is a movement borne aloft by hope. That wonderful thing with feathers, as Emily Dickinson famously wrote, "that perches in the soul, / And sings the tune without the words, / And never stops at all."[1] Isn't that what we mean by prayer, which is the language, the very grammar and syntax of hope? Especially the *Our Father*, which is the Lord's own prayer, the one He took so much trouble to tell us when the disciples first asked Jesus to teach them to pray. It is the perfect prayer of petition. What else is there but hope to sustain the mood of expectancy, of desperate desire, it awakens?

"Prayer is the little implement," Miss Dickinson tells us in another equally lovely lyric, "Through which men reach. / Where presence is denied them / They fling their speech / By means of it in God's ear." [2]We don't see God, He doesn't usually show Himself in the sphere of the sensible, yet faith tells us He is there. And you and I hope He is listening. Or so an anonymous hymnist exhorts us to do:

> We walk by faith, and not by sight;
> No gracious words we hear
> From him who spoke as none e'er spoke;
> But we believe him near.

The authentic figure of history, then, is not the corporate executive with his private plane, or the tyrant with his private army, the highly paid professional athlete, the rock superstar; but the beggar, the *mendicant*, with arms outstretched, asking for what he could never himself give. The bread of life, of meaning. "Give us this day our daily bread."

It is the task of hope to mediate all this longing and desire in relation to time, to man the creature, who necessarily exists in a kind of tension between past and future, now and then, promise and fulfillment, history and heaven. According to which I do not finally possess the perfection of my being, even as it remains the bliss I was born for, the Lord I long for. "And when I go and

---

1. *The Selected Poems of Emily Dickinson* (New York: Modern Library, 2004), poem XXXII, 20-21.
2. Ibid., poem LXXX, 49.

prepare a place for you," Jesus assures us, "I will come again and will take you to myself, that where I am you may be also" (Jn 14:3).

Perhaps I might frame it this way. On the day of my baptism, I'm told, two questions were put to me of which I've no recollection whatsoever. Which is all-right by me since in talking to other cradle Catholics I've found that they can't remember either. No one seems equal to that luminous moment when we first became a child of God, a citizen no less of eternity. As T. S. Eliot says, "We had the experience but missed the meaning . . ." In any case, here are the questions: 1. What is it that you ask of the Church of God? 2. What will the answer to that question give you that you could never on your own obtain? The answers, of course, are faith, which is the beginning, and eternal life, which is the end. And between the two, what do we have but time, the medium in which we live and move and locate our being. And, yes, hope, which is the food, the *viaticum* for the journey that will, please God, sustain our pilgrimage from time to eternity, from nature to grace, to unending glory with Him in heaven.

Meanwhile, between the eternity to which we hope someday to cross over, and the quotidian details of life on planet Earth, there falls the shadow. Despite the redeemed actuality of our moment in time, the promised presence of Jesus in the world, we are forever asking ourselves this irksome question—if Christ the Son of Justice has come, daylight having truly dawned, why then does it seem so dark? Why must I continue to suffer? Why all this pain and sorrow, dereliction and death? Not realizing, of course, that Christ doesn't come among us to take it all away, to vaporize our minds and bodies with forgetful sleep, but to fill it with His presence. Thus to deliver us from the hell of having to endure it all as sheer meaningless misery.

I bring this short reflection to a close with the following question: What if there really were a loneliness so complete and final that nothing in this world could remedy the sorrow of it? A state of abandonment so definitive that neither word nor gesture could deliver us from it? Isn't hell that very depth of loneliness where no love, no relation of real communion, can reach one in order to set free the soul of one's solitude? A life bereft of both hope and home, lacking all sense of community, or sanctuary, or escape? The Prodigal Son fated never to find his father's love but, like the Flying Dutchman, left aimless and alone forever—an eternity of grief no less—who could endure it? Who could survive a condition in which, for all eternity, one were to say to God and everyone else—I don't want to love, I don't want to be loved, I just want to be left alone?

In her memoir of the short story writer John Cheever, his daughter Susan explains the origin of the book's title, *Home Before Dark*, which includes this moving vignette on the theme of what life would be like were any of us, at the last, unable to get home before dark:[3] "My father liked to tell a story about my younger brother Fred. . . . Once, at twilight after a long summer day, my father was standing outside the house under the big elm tree that shaded the flagstones in front of the door. Fred came back from playing with some friends, worn out and tired too, and when he saw Daddy standing there he ran across the grass and threw his little boy's body into his father's arms. 'I want to go home, Daddy,' he said, 'I want to go home.' Of course he was home, just a few feet from the front door, in fact. But that didn't make any difference, as my father well understood. We all want to go home, he would say when he told this story. We all do."

But what if there were no home to go to, no one to welcome the child when he got there (when it comes to going home we are all children); indeed, our own Father telling us in words so final that nothing more will ever be said to soften the sentence: "I do not know you." Isn't there such a state as I've described already awaiting us? Death doubtless awaits us all, that nightfall through the silence of which we must someday pass and will, ineluctably, pass alone. "Someday," Karl Barth writes, "a company of men will process out to a churchyard and lower a coffin and everyone will go home; but one will not come back, and that will be me. The seal of death will be that they will bury me as a thing that is superfluous and disturbing in the land of the living."

Asked once by an interviewer what bothered him most about life, the poet Robert Lowell answered simply, "That people die."

"It is the blight man was born for," says the narrator of Hopkins' *Spring And Fall*, to the young child who has wandered innocently enough into the autumn woods where, weeping but not knowing why, she watches all the fallen leaves die. "Margaret," he asks, "are you grieving / Over Goldengrove unleaving?" Alas, he tells her, "It is the blight man was born for / It is Margaret you mourn for."

We must all die, and so, like young Margaret, we are given over to grief at the loss even of the leaves; since in nature's passing we glimpse the foreshadowing of our own. But we are not resigned to die—neither are we resigned to suffer, or to remain always alone—and so we rage, some of us, against the dying of

3. Susan Cheever's memoir of her father (Boston: Houghton Mifflin, 1984), 10–11.

the light. These things are a problem to us, an outrage even, against the heart of what it means to be human, which is the yearning to live always and in communion with others, and without pain or loss.

Pope John Paul II, in his "*Meditation on the Fourteenth Station*," describes a world literally buried beneath an immense weight of sin and death. "From the moment when man, because of sin, was banished from the tree of life, the whole earth became a burial ground. For every human being there is a tomb. A vast planet of tombs." But since we now live amid the bright shadows of the Christian Cross, whose beacon of light reaches into every corner and abyss of grief and loss, there remains an eternal springtime of hope for all who suffer. Here the real cornerstone of Christian teaching may be found. And what is that but the truth of the Event of Christ, the Suffering of Love, who wills to descend even into that state of final human loneliness and loss where death appears triumphant. There He encamps among the lost souls in order to proclaim the Father's victory. But for His free and loving descent into the horror of human desolation, there would remain but one, continuous, eternal kingdom of Death, in whose realm all men would remain helpless simply for having ceased to be. But because Christ willed to enter into that nether world, He has broken the tyranny of it for all time and eternity; only those who obdurately refuse the gift of salvation, preferring an eternity of the self-centered self, only they may not profit from His pain.

"In one of the innumerable tombs," says the pope, "scattered all over the continents of this planet of ours, the Son of God, the man Jesus Christ, conquered death with death." Only One could freely have endured so radical and complete a loneliness, the absence, seemingly forever, of the Father's presence. And that is Jesus the Christ, the very extremity of whose suffering of love has become the bedrock of our salvation. Thus we remain everlastingly grateful to the Father for Him, for His hellish descent that entitles all of us to ascend, with Him, back to the Father, back to that bliss we were born for.

Yes, hope really is the thing with feathers, provided we permit its flapping wings to carry us into the sky. May we experience the grace, that sudden galvanic jolt, to allow Jesus and His mother to wing us all the way home to heaven, and to God.

THE BEST OF TIMES
AND THE WORST OF TIMES

There are two wonderful and lasting legacies of which the Catholic Church need not be ashamed; indeed, she may trumpet them full-throatedly before the world. So surpassing is their value, so indefectible her possession of them, that neither folly nor wickedness can ever deprive her of their use. One is the Deposit of the Faith itself, which the Church is to preserve and defend because it comes to us from the Apostles, who received it from the hand of God Himself. The other patrimony is the poor and dispossessed, who likewise come to us from God, His Son having identified with them in the most profound and intimate way.

These, then, are the two abiding sources of Catholic wisdom and wealth and splendor, the repository of the Church's greatness, without which she is nothing. The story is told of a priest who witnessed St. Francis Xavier saying Mass in India four centuries ago, a somewhat unusual liturgy at which row upon row of lepers sat waiting to receive God in Holy Communion. A fastidious fellow, he appeared quite shaken by the sight, horrified by so impacted a gathering of grotesques before the altar of God. But when Father Francis motions to him to help distribute the Hosts, he is moved by a sudden grace and manages serenely to overcome his aversion, and so the story ends happily. The point it makes plunges us straightaway into the Mystery of Incarnation, whose sublime meaning the Church has always treasured, telling us never to shrink from applying it to our own lives. That in the sight of God we are all lepers, and that Jesus Christ Himself became one in order to set us free.

One of the reasons I am so drawn to the stories of Flannery O'Connor, is because they are filled with freaks. And lepers. Raving lunatics and liars, misfits of all manner of misery. Why would she want to write about such people? What is the point of filling page after page with the diseased and the demented; can so redundant a documentation of human swinishness be entirely healthy? Why this obsessive preoccupation with the violent and the grotesque? With the dark city where, she often said, the children of God lay sleeping? It was a question often put to her. Her answer was wonderfully disarming: "Because I am still able to recognize one."[1]

How does one do that? "To be able to recognize a freak," she tells us, "you have to have some conception of the whole man, and in the South (which is the region where she grew up and chose to remain) the general conception of man is still, in the main, theological . . . while the South is hardly Christ-centered, it is most certainly Christ-haunted. The Southerner, who isn't convinced of it, is very much afraid that he may have been formed in the image and likeness of God."[2] That is why the freak is given so striking a prominence in her stories, because when deployed in just that way we, the reader, are enabled to see in him "a figure for our own essential displacement," and thus "he attains some depth in literature."

Years ago as a soldier sent to Saigon, South Vietnam, my presence there proving entirely ineffectual in preventing the collapse of the American war effort, I fell in with a wonderful old priest, who managed to recruit me to help out on Sundays at the local cathedral. In order to reach the safety of the sanctuary, however, we needed to negotiate our way across a sea of human refuse . . . wave upon wave of suffering humanity—cripples, orphans, widows, beggars—those whom Christ especially identifies with in His outreach to the poor and dispossessed. What a far cry it was from the cheery suburban Catholicism of my misspent youth!

In other words, if attachment to Christ means anything, then every human being who ever existed, in whatever form of ugliness or destitution or imbecility, is to be included in the embrace of God, welcomed with open arms into the

1. See her collection of essays in *Mystery and Manners* (New York: Farrar, Straus and Giroux, 1970).
2. Ibid., 44–45.

house of God we call the Church. This is central to the whole Pauline idea of mystery, around which the Second Vatican Council had woven its tapestry of what it means to belong to Christ, to His Bride the Church. And what it consists of is this profound sense of identity between the Work and Person of Christ back in first century Palestine, and the building up of the Body of Christ in this twenty-first century post-modern world. This is the equation we simply must accept between the institution whose membership we claim today, and the reality Christ first revealed to the world He suffered to redeem more than twenty centuries ago.

Let me come at this from another perspective. You and I live in the best of times and the worst of times, to steal a great line from Charles Dickens, which he used to describe the period of the French Revolution when evil men had dug a very deep and bloody ditch. Certainly the climate of moral chaos that characterized that period, provides a number of useful parallels to our own confused age. We are living in a time of grave crisis in the Church, particularly in this country where the scandal of clerical sex abuse continues to convulse the lives of ordinary Catholic people. The nature and extent of that crisis, however, may be said to exist against a much larger backdrop of malaise and demoralization affecting the entire institutional Roman Catholic Church. It is a crisis, finally, of faith, in which more and more the choice confronting the average churchgoer is whether or not to become a mystic, or simply to go mad. Holiness, or hell? Do I aspire to become a saint (even if only to escape what Leon Bloy has called "the only sadness," to wit, not even to try to become one), or do I settle on remaining a slug? Do I turn to the *Logos* of the living God, or do I fall into some hellish pit of lunacy? Either God, or gangsterism?

Of course it is helpful to have a sense of proportion about these matters, which comes from knowing something about the past. We did not need George Santayana to tell us that those who fail to learn the lessons of the past are condemned to repeat them. Still, the historians tell us that the situation of the early Church was no doubt far worse. Our ancestors in the faith confronted far greater threats than today's newspaper editors and TV commentators are likely to unleash. After all, the enemies from the age of antiquity were ferociously bent on the destruction of the Church herself, and could no more be negotiated with than a hapless victim of terrorism could persuade his tormentors to let him go. I can well imagine the special challenges you face living among a myriad of Mormons in Utah, but so far as I can tell from local media coverage, they've not shown any sinister intention to come up here and dismantle the monastery, clapping the lot of you into dark dungeons. As for East Coast liberal media, I can tell you right now that I'd sooner face the combined hostility of *The Boston Globe* and *The New York Times* any day, than the aroused passions of the Roman mob, whose pagan customs had just been outraged by the sudden and dramatic spread of the Gospel of Jesus Christ.

Where am I going with all this? Well, it seems to me, if we possessed but half the faith of our fathers, we could perhaps all at once restore the fortunes of the Church, and, in a shot, secure the sanctification of the world. Not knowing the extent of your exposure to the period of early Christian life, it may not have crossed your minds to consider the sheer scale of the suffering ordinary Christians were subjected to; that they were not infrequently forced to endure the most barbaric and unspeakable of tortures. They were, for instance, routinely branded and burned, flayed and mutilated, blinded and castrated, crucified, too, in hideously protracted ways. So ghastly were the sufferings inflicted that I should think the prospect of merely being eaten alive by a wild beast an almost agreeable alternative. At least the ravenous animal could be expected to dispatch its victim fairly quickly.

And all this the many saints and martyrs bore with the most amazing serenity and confidence and joy; praising God and forgiving their enemies, some of whom would be converted on the spot. Think of Lawrence, the saintly deacon of Rome, his body slowly roasting on a spit, wittily instructing his tormentors that, one side being sufficiently cooked, they might turn him over! What gratitude we owe these ancient witnesses in the faith, if only because, by their sufferings, you and I are at liberty to feel smug and secure in the practice of that same faith.

What were the odds, by the way, back in the first century, for an institution as frail and fledging as the Roman Catholic Church? Its members, after all, were both few in number and not all that impressive to look at. One wonders what your average Personnel Office might say if presented with, say, a dozen illiterate fishermen who, at the first sign of trouble, take flight, leaving their leader to face torture and death alone. Indeed, one of their number turns out to have been a crook and a traitor, the exercise of whose treachery results in Christ's arrest and execution. Meanwhile, the putative leader of this entirely undistinguished group proves himself to be a liar and a coward. Not, you might say, an altogether auspicious beginning for launching a movement destined to take over the world. One thinks of Lord Acton's observation that no institution purely human could possibly have survived so many blunders; that beneath the dust of the archives, every possible corruption could be found festering before the eyes of disbelieving men. And yet, at the same time, how wonderfully God writes with crooked pencils.

I cherish in this connection the story of Cardinal Consalvi, whom Napoleon had kidnapped and taken to Paris, where he is harangued night and day on the subject of surrendering the papacy to France. And if he refused? "I shall destroy the Church!"—bellowed Napoleon. To which the chief minister of the pope replies, "Sire, in nearly two-thousand years not even we priests could accomplish that." (How hilarious that within two years of threatening the Church, poor Napoleon would find himself in exile on Elba while Consalvi and Pius VII are triumphantly restored to Rome. History, as T. S. Eliot reminds us, is full of many "cunning passages and contrived corridors.")

In quick summary, then, two things need to be remembered here: One, is the absolute uniqueness of the Catholic Thing; that Christianity is nothing less than a totally new and entirely unexpected Event in the history of the world. And, two, the fact that as Romano Guardini once put it, "in the experience of a great love, everything that happens to one becomes an event related to that love." What else can it mean but that in the saving perspective of Jesus Christ, with whom this great love affair has already been consummated, especially in the lives of the saints, everything that could possibly happen to us—of joy or pain or sorrow or disappointment, of struggle and sin and, yes, sanctity also— has already been included within the ambit of His own singular life, death, and Resurrection. It is this happy combination, it seems to me, that alone may account for, not merely the heroism of the saints and martyrs, but the sheer indestructibility of that faith to which their lives bore so eloquent and radiant a witness.

Let us ask God to give us the grace, especially of that fortitude in the faith whose source is supernatural, to go and do likewise.

SILENCE IS GOD'S FIRST LANGUAGE

St. John of the Cross, an absolutely towering figure in the history of Catholic mysticism (despite having stood less than five feet high), whose life was spent plumbing the depths of that "sounding Silence" which is but another name for God, has told us that "silence is God's first language." Which, if it were strictly true, would surely necessitate my having stopped talking a long time ago. How exactly would that justify your asking me to come all this way to talk about God? There simply must be another name for God that allows us to speak truthfully about Him. "I think that I could no longer live if I no longer heard him speak," declared Johann Adam Mohler, who felt the awe-ful resonance of God's Word eighteen hundred years after the human being Jesus returned to His Father in heaven. And how could that be if it were forbidden to us to speak His name, if He were not nameable?

So what name do we give to God that will do justice to all the perfections we rightly predicate of Him? Why not the name by which He is known by and to Himself? Word, *Logos*, who, from all eternity, speaks the Father's name, the purest wisdom and intelligibility of the Godhead itself? The Word of God is not mute. Therefore, He does not invite us to fall silent like the stones that mark the graves of the dead. Human speech is meant to imitate, to amplify even, the Voice of God, which, without beginning or end, pours forth the blessed exchanges of knowledge and love among the equal and eternal members of the Trinity. Here are depths that you and I are obliged to sound in that "intolerable wrestle / With words and meanings," of which Eliot speaks with such fierce and expressive intensity in *Four Quartets*.

> Since our concern was speech, and speech impelled us
> To purify the dialect of the tribe
> And urge the mind to aftersight and foresight . . .[1]

Of course, those that can, do; and those that cannot, well, they teach. Either one is to become a mystic, or a schoolmaster. But even the latter must not wholly be despised since the exercise of it has permitted me the great privilege of coming here among you, to bake my thirteen loaves, as it were, in your hungry presence. The quality of the bread, I suspect, has only made you hungrier. But isn't that enough for any honest wordsmith to hope for? That his own wrestle with words and meanings may succeed in quickening his audience in their search for the perfect Word, God Himself? So I thank you for your great patience and good humor in hearing me out.

In the meantime, however, this last loaf of mine is not quite ready to pop out of the oven, so I will need from you perhaps one final dollop of patience while it continues to cook. It will very shortly be done and then we can all go home. . . .

I put it to you that in trying to define our place and condition in the world, one instinctively reaches for paradoxical formulae, inasmuch as they so often provide a neat and succinct summary of who and what man is. Here then is mine. That each of us this utterly limited, finite spirit—"mounting spirit," the poet Yeats calls us, "in a bonehouse of body"—to whom nevertheless God has strangely assigned sheer unlimited, infinite destiny. In other words, I aspire to achieve absolute unending intimacy with a Being, the very perfection of whose nature—a nature, moreover, infinitely and qualitatively distant from my own—that positively prevents my ever achieving the end for which I am made. I hunger for that which I cannot have. I long for a *Logos*, an encounter with Absolute Meaning, whose language I simply cannot learn. And yet, at the same time, I realize that what it means to be human, that is, this "poor

---

1. See "Little Gidding," last of the *Four Quartets*, 141.

potsherd" of a man, who is sadly finite and contingent and therefore poor, is that I paradoxically exist in living relation to an Absolute and Eternal God. Go figure. . . .

The operative phrase here, of course, is *at the level of nature*. Because man, left to his own miserable devices, will always remain impoverished, always less than zero. We're all languishing in a ditch, as it were, but free, exhilaratingly free, to look up at the stars. And to long, with insistent, desperate desire, to commune among them. Ah, but only grace can effect so happy an outcome of nature. Only the Infinite can enable the finite to surmount the limits of its finitude. So that, as John Gillespie Magee writes in "High Flight," a stunning lyric on the longing of the human heart: ". . . with silent, lifting mind I've trod / The high untrespassed sanctity of space, / Put out my hand, and touched the face of God."[2]

There are, in the Catholic intellectual tradition, two truths about man, which no self-respecting fundamental theology can do without; they fashion the bridgework over the abyss that otherwise divides man from God. These are the two complementary orders of Creation and Covenant, Nature and Grace, History and Heaven, Time and Eternity. It is a datum fraught with an almost unbearable tension that each of us is a being both *given* and *for-given*. That man first finds himself given in the one—that is, nature—and then, the grief of sin having reduced him to shipwreck, he all at once finds himself forgiven in the other—that is, grace—thanks to the frightful events we call the Paschal Mystery. And what is that but the Passing Over of Christ into the state of being dead, which includes the deepest pain and solitude of all, that of apparent final separation from God which is the Descent into Hell.

"I first awaken to what it means to be a person," Balthasar had written in the wake of the Second Vatican Council[3] when forgetfulness of that fact had become dangerously widespread, "by the fact that Jesus Christ takes me so seriously as a spiritual person that he gives his life for my eternal salvation, and by dying buries what was evil in me with himself in hell. 'In this we have come to know his love, that he laid down his life for us; and we likewise ought to lay down our life for the brethren' (Jn 3:16)." It is all there, of course, set down so simply by one of the greatest theological minds of the modern world. Either

---

2. See my *Garlands of Grace,* 107.
3. "Meeting God in Today's World," *Concilium* 6 (1965): 20.

we love one another, or we die. And how is this to be done? As the poet Blake tells us, "by bearing the beams of love."[4]

All this is at the heart of what we in the Christian West are wont to call the *Logos Tradition*, of which the Johannine testimony of the Fourth Gospel provides the purest and most luminous expression. And the centerpiece of that tradition is the claim, both scandalous and resolute, that God has unmistakably spoken, revealing His Word to the world, indeed, in the very midst of men, in the flesh no less of human sin. So we Christians find ourselves immersed deep within the biblical world, alongside two other monotheistic peoples, for both Judaism and Islam are likewise people of the Book, of the *Word*.

The only question, of course, is to what extent these other two faith traditions remain rooted in *Logos*, their transparence genuine and deep-seated before the truth of that *Word* whose enfleshment in the human being Jesus brings salvation. Can it really be said of either Judaism or Islam that amid the idioms of each respective faith, God's *Word* achieves its fullest and most heightened expression? That here is the "still point" of ultimate unity, the place where everything else in the universe may be said to meet? It can hardly apply to the religion of Islam with its animating text, the *Koran*, having allegedly reached the prophet Mohammed through the mediation of the Archangel Gabriel. Is that even possible? Can a mere creature, never mind how seraphic its status, speak so truthfully of God that the language becomes revelatory of the sheer depth and height of God Himself? Can even an Archangel effect an interchangeability of language and *Logos*? Surely only God can speak with perfect adequacy about Himself. "For what person knows a man's thoughts," asks the Apostle Paul, "except the spirit of the man which is in him? So also no one comprehends the thoughts of God except the Spirit of God" (1 Cor 2:11). And Judaism, is it not also prevented from reaching on its own to the apogee of God's own life? Is not the whole thrust of its being trained on that which alone may complete its longing? Indeed, that which is finally transcendent to itself, but which miraculously may rescue it from the terrible grip of its own guilt? For if the Law of the Old Testament teaches us anything, it is that none of us can keep it. Who else but Christ will deliver us from the burden of sin and death?

Thus a plenitude of Revelation is needed in order precisely to parlay a relationship between God and man that can simultaneously satisfy the

---

4. From his poem "The Little Black Boy." "And we are put on earth a little space, / That we may learn to bear the beams of love."

requirements of both the divine and the human. God must, in other words, speak and show Himself exactly in those terms that do full and perfect justice to His being God; yet, at the same time, in a way that does not violate His having become fully and perfectly human, too. He can only save us by first being God, since it is clear no mere Preacher Man can save anyone; but unless He reveal Himself in a thoroughly human and humanly comprehensible way as well, why on earth would anyone wish to draw near to Him? The Mystery, if it is not to be blown apart or reduced to some human or ideological construct, has simply got to be perceived as the *Wholly Other*. At the same time, this *Otherness* may not so overwhelm the creature that he wouldn't recognize that the whole meaning of man and the world stand revealed in the human being Jesus.

Isn't this the root paradox we find at the heart of the Christian Revelation? A living God who dies? A Word unable to speak a word? "A God so intensely alive," says Balthasar, "that he can afford to be dead." Is there anything in history so sacredly terrifying as this? A God is born, and then must die—what greater collision in all the cosmos could there be? "If we no longer experience the shock of the statement," suggests Henri de Lubac, "may not the reason be that our faith has lost its cutting edge?"[5]

In a sublime poem written at age twenty-two, Chesterton declares: "I live in an age of varied powers and knowledge, / Of steam, science, democracy, journalism, art; / But when my love rises like a sea, / I have to go back to an obscure tribe and a slain man / To formulate a blessing."[6] This was the searing vision he had of slain divinity that would yet vanquish and overcome those bent on his destruction.

> When from the deeps a dying God astounded
> Angels and devils who do but die . . .

It is time we took the God of St. Paul seriously. The God who often and in varied ways spoke of old to our ancestors through the prophets; and who, in these final days, has elected to speak the entirety of His Word, His identity and work, "by a Son, whom he appointed the heir of all things, through whom also he created the ages. He reflects the glory of God and bears the very stamp of his nature. . . . having become as much superior to angels as the name he has obtained is more excellent than theirs. For to what angel did God ever say,

5. See his *The Splendor of the Church* (San Francisco: Ignatius Press, 1999), 48.
6. *Collected Works of G. K. Chesterton: Collected Poetry Part 1*, "A Blessing" (San Francisco: Ignatius Press, 1994), 30.

'You are my Son, today I have begotten you'?" (Heb 1:1–5). Certainly John of the Cross has taken him seriously, as witness this splendid text taken from his *Ascent Of Mount Carmel*, not a work for the faint of heart. "Since he has given us his Son, his only word (for he possesses no other), he spoke everything at once in this sole word—and he has no more to say . . . because what he spoke before to the prophets in parts, he has spoken all at once by giving us this All who is his Son."[7]

Where else does He speak this definitive *Word*, this perfect and eternal self-utterance of the Godhead, but in the Church of Christ, to whom He is as perfectly wedded as a husband to His Bride when, on the night of their wedding, they joyously consummate the nuptial meaning of the body? "When I start to speak of her," exclaims Augustine, "I cannot stop."[8]

Well, I'm afraid I must, at least in a minute or two . . .

How beautifully Bishop Jacques-Bénigne Bosseut put it when he pronounced: "The Church is Jesus Christ spread abroad and communicated."[9] She is thus the fire of a single furnace, which is the Heart of Christ, the heart of the world. Or as St. Cyprian put it back in the third century with characteristic, uncompromising rigor: "You cannot have God as Father unless you agree to have the Church as Mother."[10] In clinging to God and His mother, we do not understand ourselves to be members of a dysfunctional family.

Or, again, St. Augustine, another superb North African Churchman, born in what today is Algeria, insisting that, "the Church of today is the kingdom of Christ and the Kingdom of Heaven." What else can that mean but that in beholding her we truly behold Him. It is all in St. Paul, of course, and not only in the Letters but in the life. "I am Jesus, whom you are persecuting," God told him on that fateful day when, en route to Damascus in search of fresh meat to devour, he is rudely unhorsed and thereupon sees the light. Like that charming story we are told of St. Martin of Tours, espying a beggar in the dead of winter, splitting his cloak at once in order that he might share the warmth, only to have Jesus Himself appear to him in a dream that night dressed in the other half of the cloak. Is this not the Mystery we invoke at every Mass? "By the Mystery of this water and wine may we come to share in the divinity of Christ, who humbled himself to share in our humanity."

7. Cited by Pope Benedict XVI in his Post-Synodal Apostolic Exhortation on The Word of God *Verbum Domini* (September 30, 2010), no. 14.
8. Cited by Henri de Lubac in *Splendor of the Church*, 46..
9. Cited by de Lubac in Ibid., 48.
10. Cited by de Lubac in Ibid., 265–266.

I think, unlike Augustine—who was, after all, a bishop and a doctor of the Church—I had better stop.

Let us ask Jesus, who is head of the Church we dare to join our lives to as bride and body, to fill us with such power and presence of Himself that we might carry Him, following this retreat, to the very ends of the earth.

AFTERWORD

Suppose you were to drive a stake right through the heart of Christianity. Go ahead. Just do it. Would the resulting incision separate the sheep from the goats? Would a clean surgical strike, as it were, straight down the middle, forcing everyone to the margins, in effect drive the wicked and worldly to one extreme, the upright and godly to the other? Is that the line of division, do you think, prescribed by faith?

Because, from a certain angle, it does look wonderfully, seductively simple to pull off. Neat as a pin, simple as soup. At least that's how it looks on paper. In the real world, of course, none of us would survive the pruning shears. If you insist on a paradigm of membership in Christ's Body so pure that only saints need enroll, the unwashed masses having sunk too deep into the morass of sin for God to salvage, then you might as well write off the entire human race as hopelessly reprobate. Where then will you locate the love and the mercy of Almighty God? It would have nothing to work on.

Sadly, there are many who profess to being sick unto death of the Church they belong to. So what's stopping them from simply going out and establishing a better one, indeed, a Church so perfect that only the virtuous need apply? Would that please them? Bear in mind, however, that from the first instant of they're having founded such a thing, all that vaunted perfection would be diminished by their membership in it.

"I would hate to belong to a club," Groucho Marx once famously quipped, "that would have someone like me as a member." Thank God the standards of His Son are far less exacting. Criteria for admission to Christ's Church are so loose as to appear positively promiscuous, that is, anybody can join.

So what is the litmus test? Well, have you got a heart? Does it beat with the need and the desire to be happy? What about beauty, or peace, or joy, or love—do these immortal longings define your life? Do they float your boat? Does the hope in your heart spring eternal? Then why aren't you baptized? Do you want to become a New Creature, or not?

How freeing the insight of that incomparable Christian, Charles Peguy, who often told us that at the heart of the Catholic Thing, which for a thousand and more years formed the culture of Christendom, provision must be made both for the saint and the sinner. In other words, when you come to the real line of demarcation between Church and world, the fault line does not run between the righteous and the wicked, with men of virtue standing athwart those of vice. No, the dividing line is always Christ, whose sole and consuming passion is to be with sinners in order to transform them into saints.

"When God looks at a sinner," Father Vincent McNabb used to say, "he is no longer a sinner; he used to be a sinner."

I so often had to remind myself of that fact, and the consolation it brought, during the heady days of my stay among the holy men of Utah. Because, for all the distance separating me from these godly specimens, we remained nevertheless creatures of the same God, annealed to the same Christ by virtue of our common Baptism. We therefore stood equally in need of the medicine of God's mercy. Every hour of every day. Could it be that what really distinguishes me from them is that, unlike the monks, I just don't ask nearly so often for it?

In a letter sent to a woman who, despite having just turned Catholic, was already determined on becoming an ex-Catholic (presumably she'd stayed just long enough to become acquainted with the sins of other Catholics), Flannery O'Connor wrote, prophetically:

> I think that the Church is the only thing that is going to make
> the terrible world we are coming to endurable; the only thing
> that makes the Church endurable is that it is somehow the
> Body of Christ and that on this we are fed.

Isn't that wonderful? I find that it expresses with great wit and precision, exactly the attitude we are to have if the offer of salvation—bestowed by Christ, imparted by His Church—is to make any difference in our lives. And because of that mysterious bond we share with the whole Body of Christ, which is the Church we belong to, we can be full of confidence and trust that the event of Christ will infallibly take place wherever the People of God gather to celebrate the Mystery. What a joy it was to find Christ in so rich and intense a way amid the mountains and the monks of Utah. I am utterly grateful for their many kindnesses to me that blessed week, not the least being the invitation itself to come and speak to them of Christ.

FIDELITY. HOLINESS. CHARITY.

Three pillars on which the work of Catholics United for the Faith rests.

Fidelity to the wisdom of Scripture and Tradition is essential to our mission—which is and always has been to "support, defend, and advance the efforts of the teaching Church."

Holiness, friendship with God, is the reason we strive to be faithful to the Church which Christ has established. Our goal is to help Catholics become, ever more perfectly, the image of God.

Charity is our aim in all we do, whether in our work with bishops and priests, our outreach in dioceses and parishes, and our relations with fellow believers and non-believers alike.

Catholics United for the Faith (CUF) is a lay apostolate founded in 1968 to equip the laity to know and live out their calling as followers of Christ. We provide formation through our trusted resources to help Catholics of every age, vocation, and state of life both live and proclaim the fullness of truth.

Our resources include:

- The award winning *Lay Witness* magazine
- A research department to answer our CUF members' most pressing questions about the faith
- The CUF website (cuf.org) which contains thousands of articles, audio tracks, and information useful to the faithful
- Emmaus Road Publishing, our publishing arm which provides books, Bible studies, and more to help Catholics better know and live their faith
- Faith Facts, or succinct tracts on commonly asked questions answered with accuracy and fidelity to the Church's teachings.

"This is our definitive, deepest and greatest motivation, the ultimate reason and meaning behind all we do: the glory of the Father which Jesus sought at every moment of his life."
—Pope Francis, *Evangelii gaudium*

If your desire is to glorify the Father by fully living your Catholic faith, stand with us.
Visit www.cuf.org for more information.

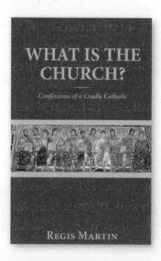